Understanding
Google Sheets

Kevin Wilson

Elluminet Press

www.elluminetpress.com

Understanding Google Sheets

iStock.com/golibo, PeopleImages, ymgerman. Photo 130859010 © Kaspars Grinvalds - Dreamstime.com. Photo 103557713 © Konstantin Kolosov - Dreamstime.com. Yuri Arcurs via Getty Images, Cover Image by Chris Bardgett / Alamy Stock Photo, iStockPhoto elenabs

Publisher: Elluminet Press
Director: Kevin Wilson
Lead Editor: Steven Ashmore
Technical Reviewer: Mike Taylor, Robert Ashcroft
Copy Editors: Joanne Taylor, James Marsh
Proof Reader: Mike Taylor
Indexer: James Marsh
Cover Designer: Kevin Wilson

eBook versions and licenses are also available for most titles. Any source code or other supplementary materials referenced by the author in this text is available to readers at www.elluminetpress.com/resources

For detailed information about how to locate your book's resources, go to www.elluminetpress.com/resources

Table of Contents

About the Author

With over 20 years' experience in the computer industry, Kevin Wilson has made a career out of technology and showing others how to use it. After earning a master's degree in computer science, software engineering, and multimedia systems, Kevin has held various positions in the IT industry including graphic & web design, building & managing corporate networks, training, and IT support.

He currently serves as senior writer and director at Elluminet Press Ltd, he periodically teaches computer science at college in South Africa and serves as an IT trainer in England. His books have become a valuable resource among the students in England, South Africa and our partners in the United States.

Kevin's motto is clear: "If you can't explain something simply, then you haven't understood it well enough." To that end, he has created a series of textbooks, in which he breaks down complex technological subjects into smaller, easy-to-follow steps that students and ordinary computer users can put into practice.

Google Sheets

Google Sheets was originally called XL2Web, a web based spreadsheet program created by a company called 2Web Technologies, which Google acquired in 2006 and developed it into Google Sheets.

Google Sheets is a spreadsheet included in the web-based Google Docs Editors Suite developed by Google.

Google Sheets runs in a web browser on Windows and Mac platforms. There is also an app available for Android tablets and phones, as well as for iPhone or iPad.

There are collaborative features allowing teams and multiple users to work on projects together in real time from locations all over the world.

To use Google Sheets, you will need a Google Account.

Google Sheets is a web application meaning it runs on the internet and is available on multiple platforms such as MacOS or Windows 10, as well as Linux and Chromebook.

Google Sheets is also available as an app for iPhone/iPad and Android tablets and phones. You can download these from the app stores on these platforms.

The spreadsheets you create are saved onto Google Drive which is a cloud based storage service that allows you to access your files from anywhere and on any device.

There are also tools to convert documents to other formats such as Microsoft Excel, Open Office Calc, as well as PDF documents. This allows you to send these documents to other people who might be using other operating systems and software.

Chapter 1: Google Sheets

Multiple users can open a spreadsheet at the same time using Google Sheets' collaboration features. These other users can be anywhere in the world with an internet connection.

Here, you can see two other people editing a spreadsheet in real time. The edits other users are working on are indicated with their name tag.

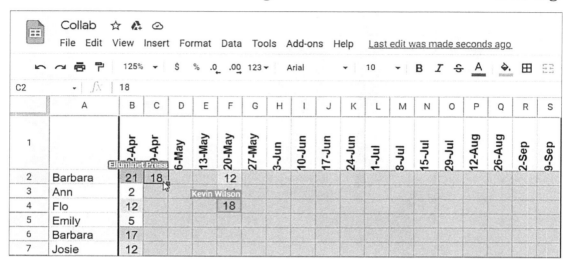

You can also expand Google Doc's functionality with addons. These add ons are developed mostly by third party developers.

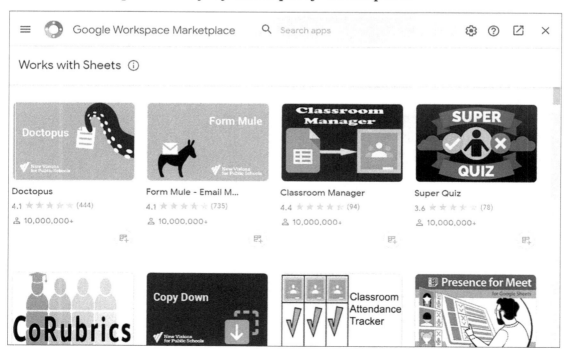

You'll find addons for spreadsheet specific features such as data analysis, charting, as well as document export and quizzes.

Google Sheets also includes various data analysis tools such as pivot tables...

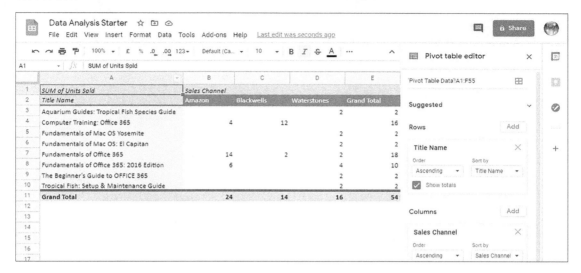

... as well as various mathematical functions and formulas.

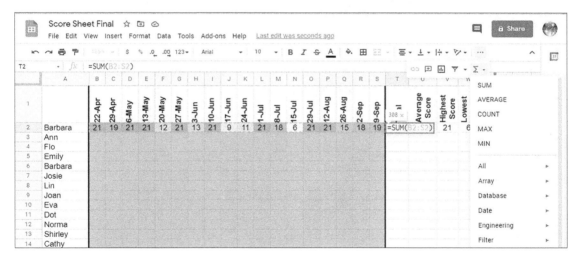

You'll also find more advanced macro recorders and script editors.

Getting Started

In this chapter we'll take a look at getting started with Google Sheets using a web browser such as Google Chrome. You can also use Microsoft Edge if you're on a PC or Safari if you're on a Mac.

Have a look at the video resources section. Open your web browser and navigate to the following website.

`videos.tips/starting-googlesheets`

Creating a Google Account

If you use Gmail you will already have a Google Account. If this is the case, you don't need to create a new Google Account so you can skip this step.

If you don't have an account, you can create one online before you start. To do this, open your web browser and browse to the following page.

accounts.google.com/signup

Fill in your name in the first two fields, then under 'username', type in the name you want to appear in your email address. This can be a nickname or your full name. The name must be unique, so if someone else has already taken the name, you'll need to choose a new one or add a couple of numbers. Google will tell you if the username you entered has already been used.

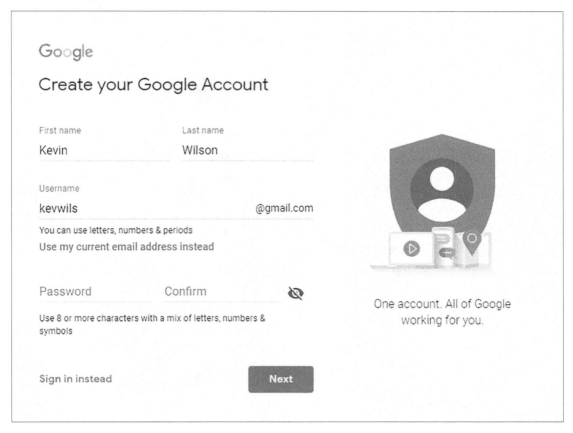

Enter the password you want to use in the 'password' field, then type it again to confirm it in the 'confirm' field.

Click 'next'.

Sign In

Once you have your Google Account, you can sign in. Google Sheets will run in any web browser, however Google recommend using their own Chrome browser. To start Google Sheets, open your browser, go to

`sheets.google.com`

Sign in with your Google Account email address and password.

Once you sign in, you'll land on the Google Sheets start or home screen.

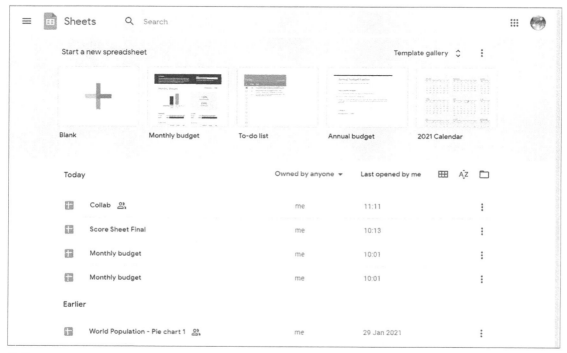

Get Started

Let's take a closer look at the home screen.

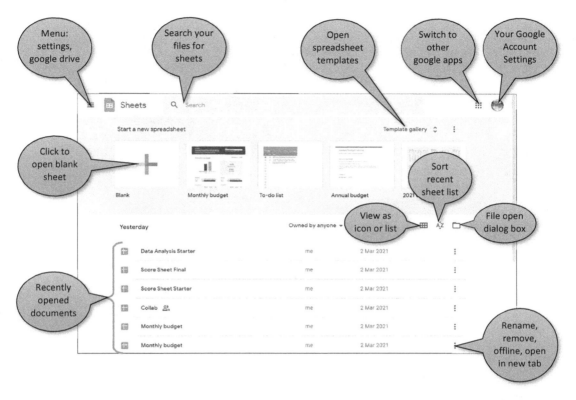

From here, you can create a new sheet. You can do this by selecting a blank sheet.

You can select a template from the pre-designed projects if you want to create a to-do list, monthly budget, time sheet, or class grade book. To use a template, click 'template gallery', then select a template.

In this example, we're going to start a spreadsheet from scratch, so select 'blank'.

Menus & Toolbars

When you open a new sheet, you'll see a some icons along the top and bottom...

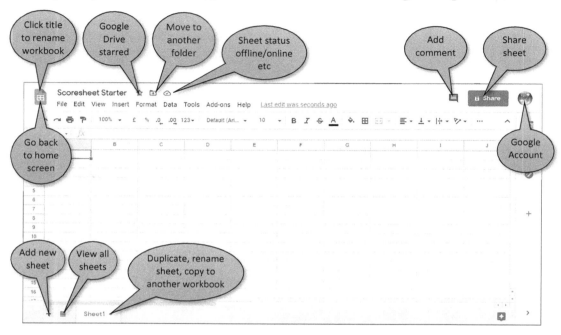

Under the sheet title, there are pull-down menus: file, edit, etc. You will find various commands here for dealing with files, editing your spreadsheet, as well as borders, formulas, functions and tools for grammar and spelling.

Menu	Command
File	New file, share, open, import, email, download, and print.
Edit	Cut, copy, paste, find, delete row/column
View	Freeze panes, show formulaes, zoom, hidden sheets
Insert	Chart, image, drawing, form, function, link, note, new sheet
Format	Theme, number, font size, align, merge cells, text wrap/rotation, conditional formatting
Data	Sort, filter, slicer, data validation, pivot table
Tools	Create form, appsheet, script editor, macros, spelling

Underneath the menus along the top, you'll see a toolbar:

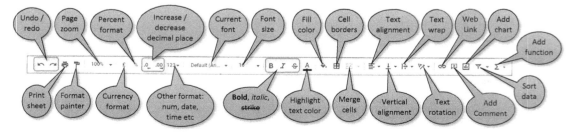

This is where you'll find your formatting tools, font colours and sizes.

What is a Spreadsheet?

A spreadsheet is made up of cells each identified by a reference. The reference is made up by using the column, eg C, and the row, eg 9

[COLUMN] [ROW]

So the highlighted cell in the example below, would be C9, as it is in column C and row 9.

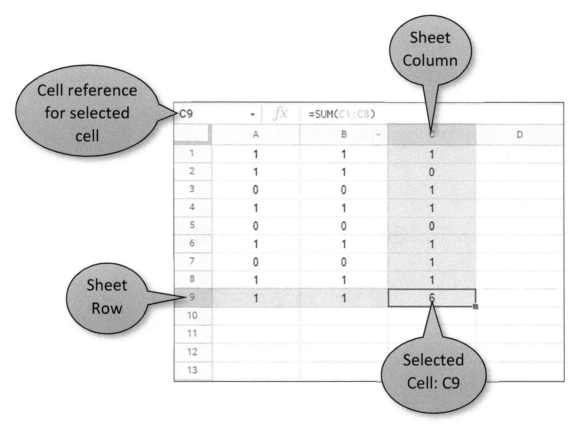

You can also select multiple cells at the same time. A group of cells is called as a cell range.

You can refer to a cell range, using the cell reference of the first cell and the last cell in the range, separated by a colon.

Here in the example, I've selected the range from cell A1 to cell C9.

[FIRST CELL in RANGE] : [LAST CELL in RANGE]

Download Google Chrome

Google Chrome is a fast and streamlined browser that is a good alternative to Microsoft Edge. To use Google Chrome, you'll first need to download it.

Open your current web browser and navigate to the following website. You can download Google Chrome from here.

`www.google.com/chrome`

Click the blue 'download chrome' button on the web page.

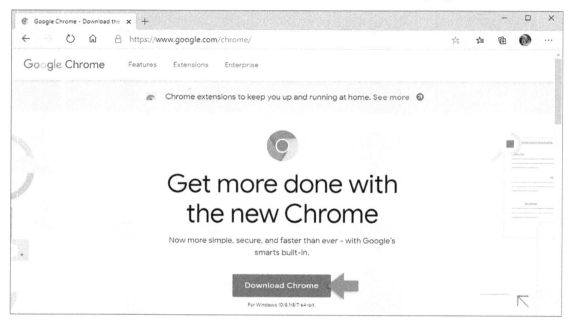

Click 'open' when prompted by your browser then follow the on screen instructions to install Chrome.

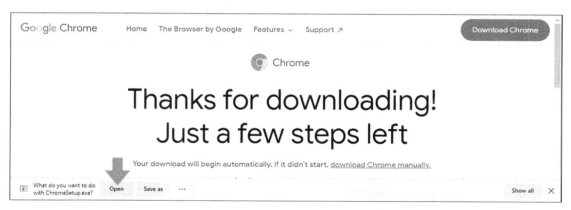

If you don't see the prompt, go to your downloads folder and double click 'chromesetup.exe'.

You'll find Chrome on your start menu and on your desktop. Click the chrome icon to start.

Once you open Chrome, sign in with your Google Account email address and password. Click the profile icon on the top right. Then click 'turn on sync.

Enter your Google Account email address and password when prompted. Click 'next'.

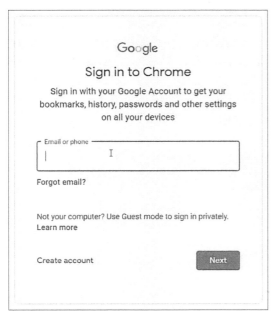
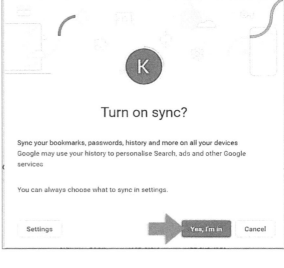

Click 'yes I'm in' to synchronise your data across all your devices. This is useful if you use your account on your iPad, phone, chromebook as well as on windows 10 or mac.

Building Spreadsheets

In this section, we'll take a look at building and formatting spreadsheets.

Before we begin, throughout this section, we will be using the resource files. You can download these files from the following website.

`videos.tips/building-googlesheets`

Go down to the files section and click the icons to download the documents to the documents folder on your PC, then import them into google sheets.

Creating a New Workbook

A workbook is a collection of spreadsheets, you can have more than one sheet per workbook. To create a new blank workbook, click 'file' on the top left of your screen.

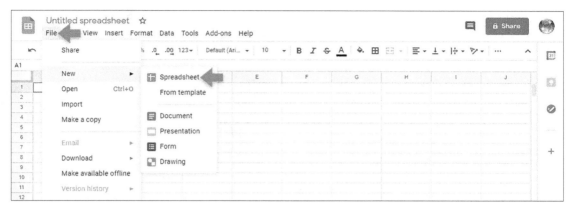

Go down to 'new', then select 'spreadsheet' from the slideout menu. You'll see a blank spreadsheet appear, where you can start to enter your data.

If you're on the home or start screen, click on 'blank' to open a new spreadsheet.

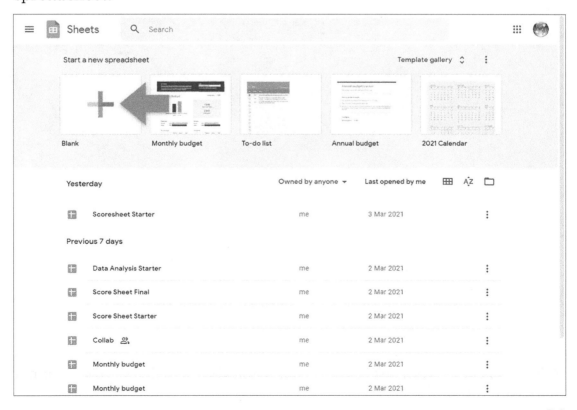

Entering Data

In this example we are doing a basic scoring sheet. To enter data, click on the cell you want, then type in the data.

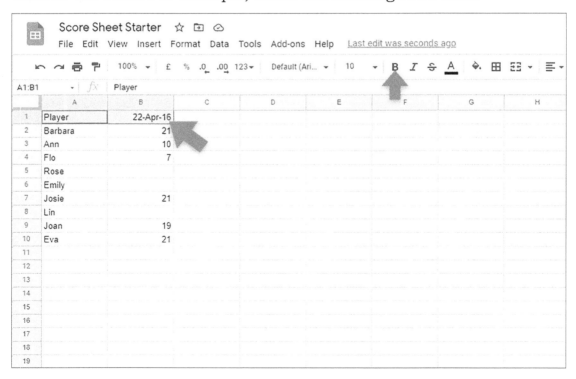

Simple Text Formatting

Sometimes it improves the readability of your spreadsheet to format the data in the cells. For example, make the heading rows bold.

Select the cells with your mouse, then click the 'bold' icon on the toolbar along the top of the screen.

Text Orientation

Now because the headings are quite long and take up a lot of space, you can change the orientation of the headings to read vertically instead of horizontally. This helps save space and looks better when printed on a page.

To do this, select the cells you want to change the orientation of, eg the headings. From the toolbar, select the 'text rotation' icon.

From the drop down menu select an orientation. You can rotate your text 45° to the left, or 45° to the right. You can stack your text vertically, or you can rotate your text up or down.

You can also rotate your text an arbitrary angle. Type the number of degrees into the field on the right hand side of the drop down box.

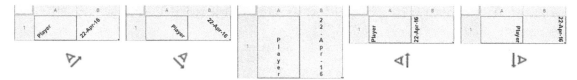

Zero degrees is horizontal text. Remember when entering an angle of rotation, a positive number will rotate the text counter-clockwise, a negative number will rotate the text clockwise. The text is rotated around a point on the left hand side next to the first letter.

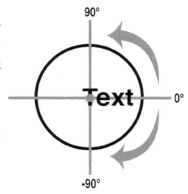

You will see the headings are now oriented vertically.

Give it a try and see what happens.

Resizing Columns and Rows

To resize a column, hover your mouse pointer over one of the column dividing lines. You'll see your mouse pointer turn into a double sided arrow. Now, click and drag the column divider to resize, as shown below.

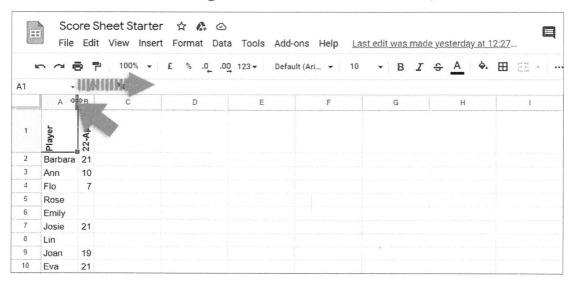

Similarly with row widths. Click on the row divider, once your mouse pointer turns into a double sided arrow, click and drag the row divider to resize.

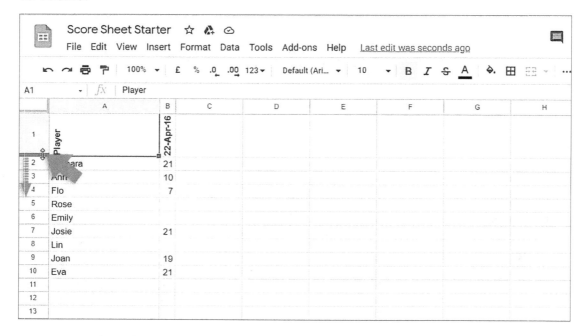

You can also double click on these lines to automatically size the row or column to the data that is in the cell.

Inserting Rows & Columns

To insert a row between Flo and Rose, right click with your mouse on the row Rose is in. In this case row 5.

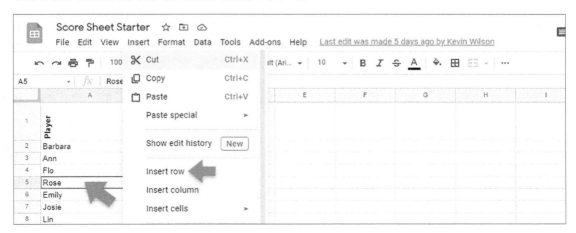

From the popup menu, 'click insert row'. This will insert a blank row above Rose. Remember, the new row is always added above the one selected.

To insert a column it is exactly the same procedure, except you select a column instead of a row. Here, I'm inserting a column between the player column and the first date.

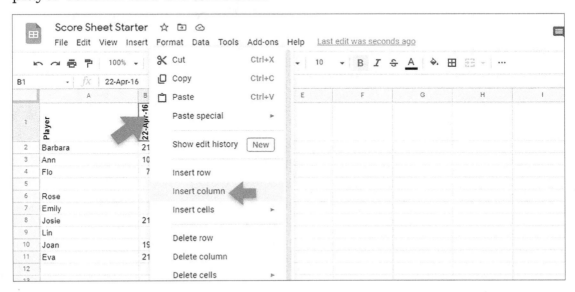

Remember, the new column is always added to the left of the one selected.

To delete a row or column, right click on it, then select 'delete row' to delete a row, or select 'delete column' to delete a column.

Cut, Copy & Paste

You can copy and paste a cell or cell range, and paste it into another worksheet/workbook or in a different location on the same worksheet.

First, select the cells you want to copy, and from your home ribbon, click copy. In this example, I'm going to select the cells A1:B10, as highlighted below.

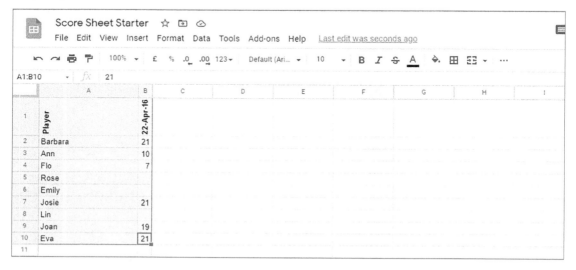

Right click where you want the cells to be copied to, then select 'paste' from the popup menu. I'm going to paste the cells starting from E1.

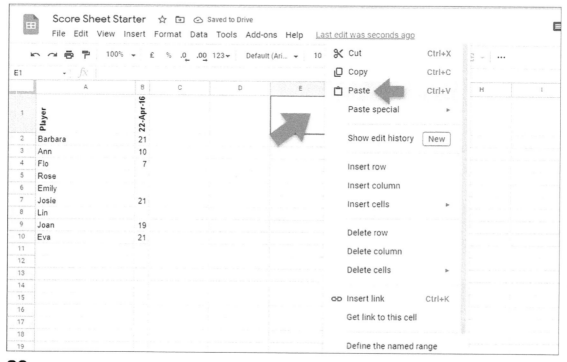

By default, Google Sheets pastes everything copied from the selected cells. Sometimes you only want to paste certain things, such as formatting, or just the text or just the formulas. You can do this with the 'paste special' feature. To find 'paste special', go down to 'paste special' in the popup menu.

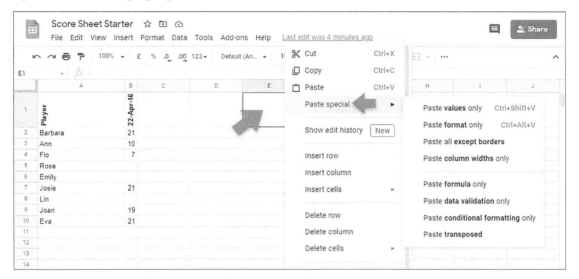

Select an option from the slideout menu.

Paste values only pastes the visible values from the copied cells and nothing else - ie no formatting, borders or formulas.

Paste format only pastes the cell formatting and nothing else - ie no text or formulas from the copied cells.

Paste all except borders pastes everything from the copied cells except the cell borders.

Paste column widths only pastes in the column width from the copied cells - ie resizes the pasted columns to match the copied columns.

Paste formula only pastes the formulas contained in a copied cells rather than the results of the formulas themselves.

Paste data validation only pastes the data validation rules from the copied cells ignoring the existing formatting, formulas, or text.

Paste conditional formatting only pastes in the conditional formatting rules from the copied cells.

Paste transposed pastes a rotated version of the copied cells, meaning you can copy a column and paste it as a row and vice versa.

Using 'cut' is exactly the same, except select 'cut' from the home ribbon, instead of copy. The cut command moves the selected cells rather than copying them.

Sorting Data

To quick sort your data, click on a cell in the column you want to sort the data by. In this example, I want to sort the data by total score so I can see who won this year's player of the year.

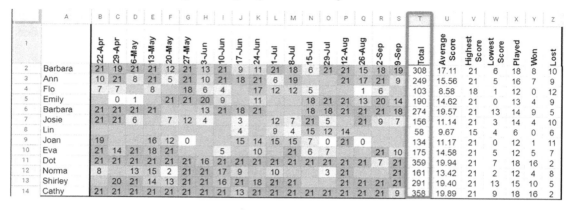

	22-Apr	29-Apr	6-May	13-May	20-May	27-May	3-Jun	10-Jun	17-Jun	24-Jun	1-Jul	8-Jul	15-Jul	29-Jul	12-Aug	26-Aug	2-Sep	9-Sep	Total	Average Score	Highest Score	Lowest Score	Played	Won	Lost
Barbara	21	19	21	21	12	21	13	21	9	11	21	18	6	21	21	15	18	19	308	17.11	21	6	18	8	10
Ann	10	21	8	21	5	21	10	21	18	21	6	19			21	17	21	9	249	15.56	21	5	16	7	9
Flo	7	7		8			18	6	4		17	12	12	5			1	6	103	8.58	18	1	12	0	12
Emily		0	1		21	21	20	9		11			18	21	21	13	20	14	190	14.62	21	0	13	4	9
Barbara	21	21	21	21			13	21	18	21			18	18	21	21	21	18	274	19.57	21	13	14	9	5
Josie	21	21	6		7	12	4		3		12	7	21	5		21	9	7	156	11.14	21	3	14	4	10
Lin							4				9	4	15	12	14				58	9.67	15	4	6	0	6
Joan	19			16	12	0			15	14	15	15	7	0	21	0			134	11.17	21	0	12	1	11
Eva	21	14	21	18	21			5		10			21	6	7		21	10	175	14.58	21	5	12	5	7
Dot	21	21	21	21	21	21	16	21	21	21	21	21	21	21	21	21	7	21	359	19.94	21	7	18	16	2
Norma	8		13	15	2	21	21	17	9		10			3	21			21	161	13.42	21	2	12	4	8
Shirley		20	21	14	13	21	21	16	21	18	21	21			21	21	21	21	291	19.40	21	13	15	10	5
Cathy	21	21	21	21	21	21	21	21	13	21	21	21	21	21	21	21	21	9	358	19.89	21	9	18	16	2

Since this spreadsheet has a title row (ie row 1), you'll first need to freeze the top row, otherwise Google Sheets will try and sort the title row. This isn't what we want, we just want to sort the players scores (from row 2). To freeze row 1, click on the 'view' menu, go down to 'freeze', then select '1 row' from the slideout menu. This freezes one row from the top.

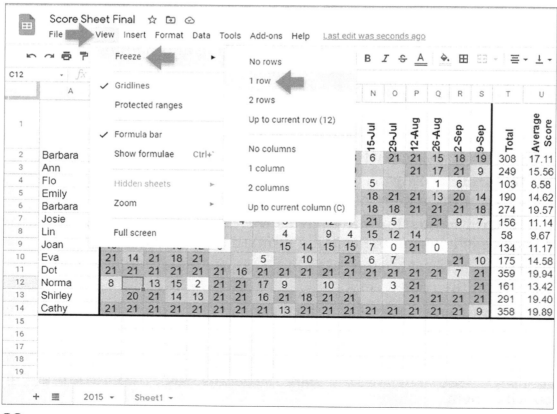

In this example, we want to sort the data by total score. Total score is in column T. Hover your mouse pointer over the column header, you'll see a small down arrow appear. Click on this arrow.

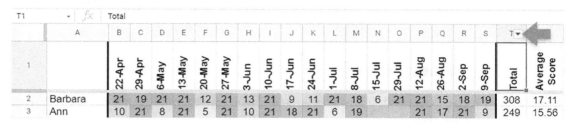

From the popup menu, go down to the sorting section. You'll see two options. Select 'sort sheet A - Z' to sort into ascending order - ie starting with the smallest value. Select 'sort sheet Z - A' to sort into descending order - ie largest value at the top.

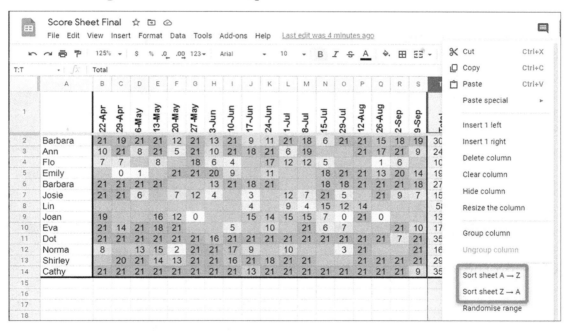

In this case I want the largest value on the top... So I'm going to select 'sort sheet Z - A'.

	A	B 22-Apr	C 29-Apr	D 6-May	E 13-May	F 20-May	G 27-May	H 3-Jun	I 10-Jun	J 17-Jun	K 24-Jun	L 1-Jul	M 8-Jul	N 15-Jul	O 29-Jul	P 12-Aug	Q 26-Aug	R 2-Sep	S 9-Sep	T Total	U Average Score	V Highest Score	W Lowest Score	X Played	Y Won	Z Lost
2	Dot	21	21	21	21	21	21	16	21	21	21	21	21	21	21	21	21	7	21	359	19.94	21	7	18	16	2
3	Cathy	21	21	21	21	21	21	21	21	13	21	21	21	21	21	21	21	21	9	358	19.89	21	9	18	16	2
4	Barbara	21	19	21	21	12	21	13	21	9	11	21	18	6	21	21	15	18	19	308	17.11	21	6	18	8	10
5	Shirley		20	21	14	13	21	21	16	21	18	21	21			21	21	21	21	291	19.40	21	13	15	10	5
6	Barbara	21	21	21	21			13	21	18	21			18	18	21	21	21	18	274	19.57	21	13	14	9	5
7	Ann	10	21	8	21	5	21	10	21	18	21	6	19			21	17	21	9	249	15.56	21	5	16	7	9
8	Emily		0	1		21	21	20	9		11			18	21	21	13	20	14	190	14.62	21	0	13	4	9

Looks like Dot won this one, with 359 points.

Filtering Data

Filtering comes in useful for larger spreadsheets with a lot of data to go through. Here in this example, I have a list of book sales in their various sales channels. There is a lot of data to go though.

Filter by Values

First, freeze the top row. This prevents the header row from being filtered with the rest of the data.

Next, select the range of cells you want to filter. I'm going to filter columns A - C.

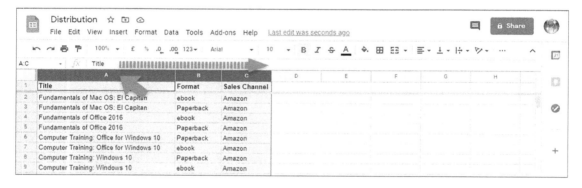

Click on the 'data' menu, then select 'create a filter'.

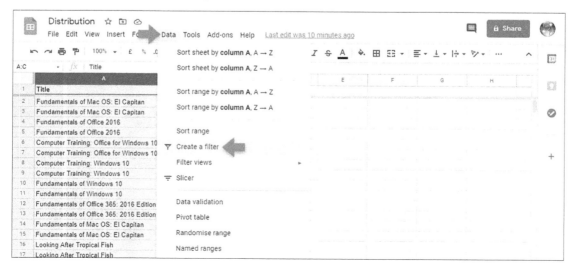

Along the top of your selected cells, you'll see a filter icon on the top right of each column.

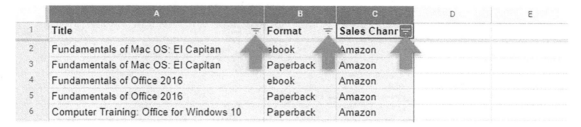

Click the drop-down arrow for the column you want to filter. In this example, I'm going filter my data by sales channel in column C.

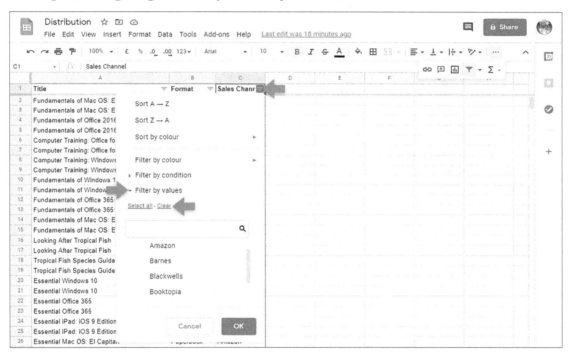

Expand the 'filter by values' section, then click 'clear' to remove all of the selections.

Now, select the values you want to filter. In this example, I want to show all sales through the Blackwells sales channel. So I'd select 'blackwells' from the list. Click 'ok' when you're done.

Chapter 3: Building Spreadsheets

Here you'll see the filtered data.

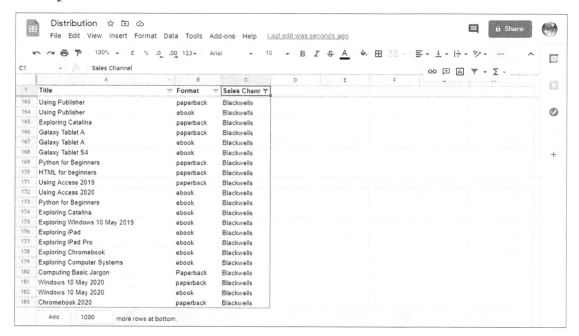

If you wanted to further filter the data, we could show only paperback titles in this sales channel. To do this, select the filter icon next to 'format'.

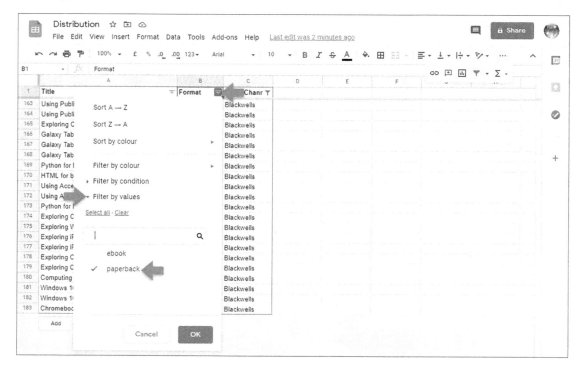

Click 'ok' when you're done.

Filter by Condition

You can also filter your data using various conditions. You can filter data containing certain text, greater or smaller than a particular number, or you can add custom formulas.

To do this, first freeze the top row. This prevents the header row from being filtered with the rest of the data.

Next, select the range of cells you want to filter. I'm going to filter columns A - C.

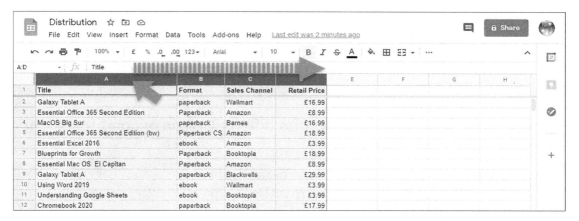

Click on the 'data' menu, then select 'create a filter'.

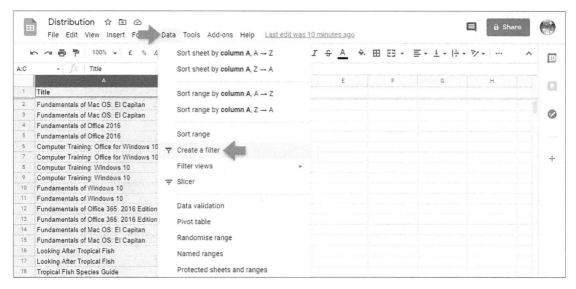

Click the drop-down arrow for the column you want to filter. In this example, I'm going filter my data by retail price in column D.

Now, I want to find all books with prices that are less than £9.99. To do this, I need to add a filter condition. So, expand the 'filter by condition' section, then select the drop down box 'none'.

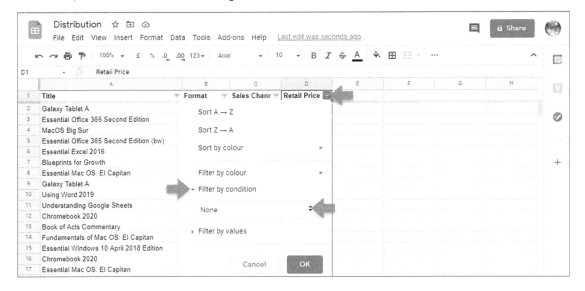

From the list, you can select various different types of conditions. Let's take a look at what they mean.

Cell **is empty** returns rows whose cells don't contain any data (such as text, numbers, or formulas in them).

Cell **is not empty** returns rows whose cells contain data.

Text does not contain returns rows whose cells do not contain the data you enter into the 'value field'. This could be numeric, text, or a symbol .

Text contains returns rows whose cells contain the data you enter into the 'value field'. This could be numeric, text, or a symbol.

Text starts with returns rows whose cells contain the data that starts with the text you enter into the 'value field'.

You don't need to use wildcards with these...

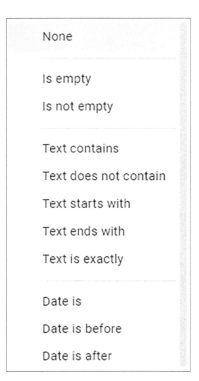

Text ends with returns rows whose cells contain the data that ends with the text you enter into the 'value field'.

Text is exactly returns rows whose cells exactly match the text you enter into the 'value field'.

You can filter **dates** that come after or before the date you enter into the 'value field'.

You can filter **values** that are greater than, less than or equal to a value you enter into the 'value field'.

Going back to our example, I want to find all books with prices that are less than £9.99. So, from the popup menu, I'd select 'less than'.

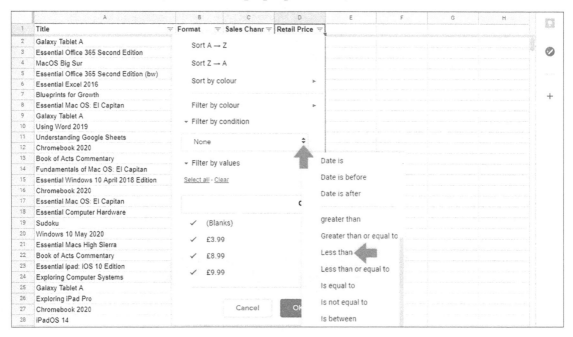

Enter the condition (in this case 9.99) into the value field. Click 'ok'.

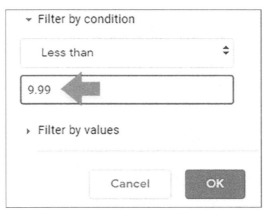

Saving Filters

To save your current filter, click the 'data' menu, go down to 'filter views', then select 'save as filter view'.

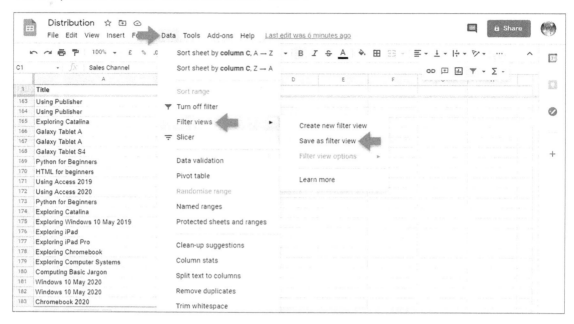

Give the filter a meaningful name...

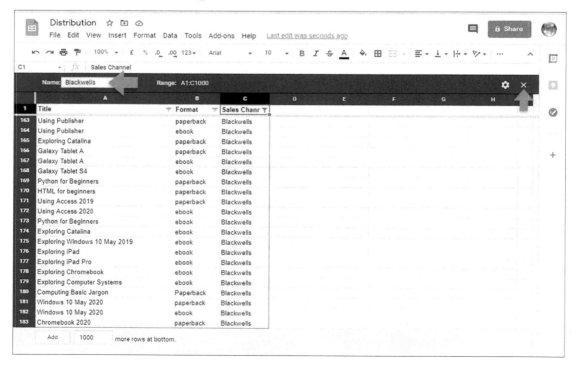

Click the 'x' on the top right to close.

Show a Saved Filter

First, open the spreadsheet. Select the 'data' menu, go down to 'filter views'.

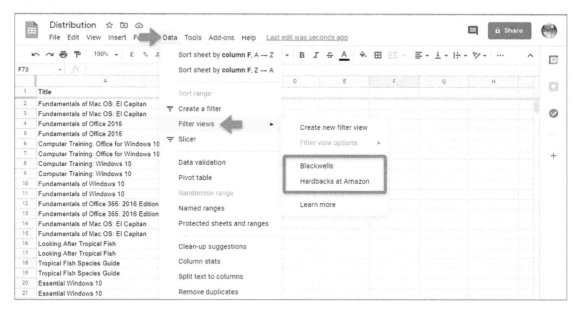

In the middle of the slideout menu, you'll see all your saved filters. Select a filter to apply it to your spreadsheet.

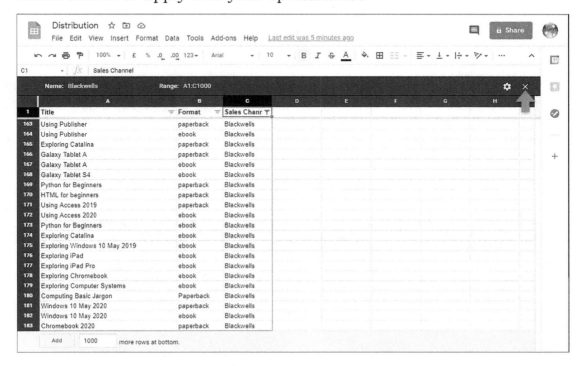

To close a filter view, click the x icon on the top right.

Remove a Filter

To remove a filter, click on the 'data' menu, then select 'turn off filter'.

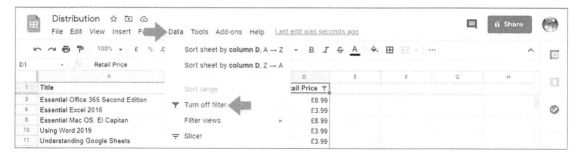

This will remove any applied filters to your spreadsheet.

Delete Saved Filter

To delete a saved filter, click on the 'data' menu, go down to 'filter views', then from the slideout menu, select the one you want to delete.

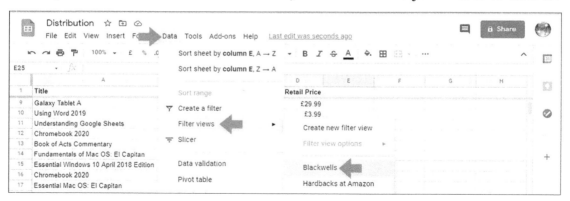

Click on the cog icon on the top right of the filter display.

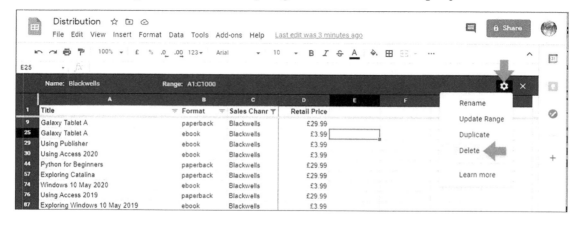

Select 'delete' from the drop down menu.

Formatting your Spreadsheet

To emphasise certain parts of your spreadsheet such as totals or headings, you can apply borders and shading to cells or groups of cells.

Horizontal Cell Alignment

This helps to align your data inside your cells to make it easier to read. To do this, highlight the cells you want to apply the alignment to, then select the alignment icon from the toolbar. *If you don't see the icon, click the three dots icon on the right of the toolbar.*

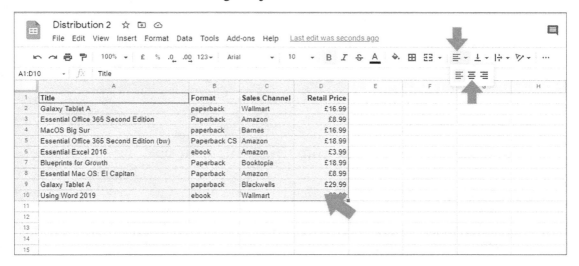

From the drop menu, select an alignment: left, center, or right.

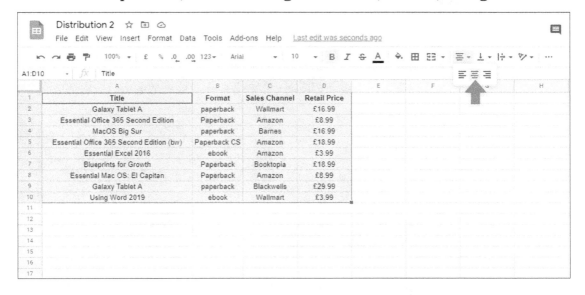

Here, I've aligned all the columns to the center.

Vertical Cell Alignment

You can also align text vertically in a cell: top, middle, or bottom. Select your cells, then from the toolbar, click on the vertical align icon.

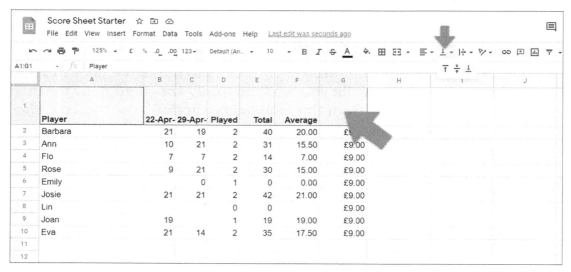

Select top, middle, or bottom from the drop down box.

Text Wrap

You can also rotate text in a cell. Select your cells, then from the toolbar, click on the rotate text icon.

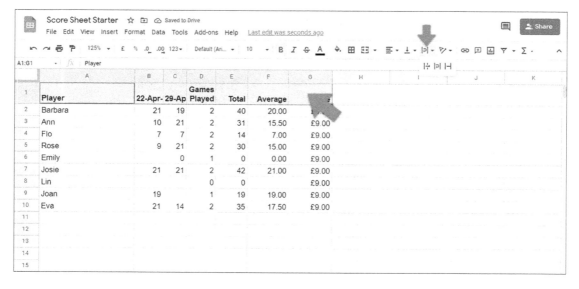

Select a wrap mode. Overflow allows text in one cell to overflow into adjacent cells. Wrap mode wraps the text to fit inside the cell. Clip mode clips the text to fit the cell and hides the rest.

Text Format

As well as aligning the text inside your cell, you can apply bold or italic effects to make certain parts such as headings stand out. You can also change the font and size.

To do this in our spreadsheet highlight the headings ('22-Apr' to 'Fee Paid').

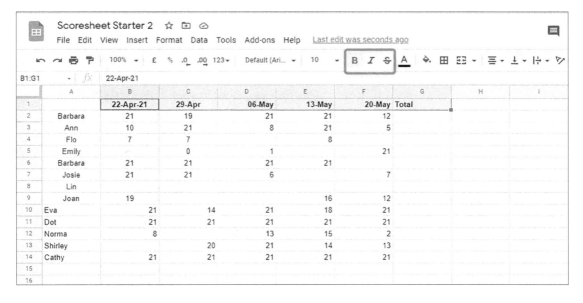

You'll see three text formatting icons on the toolbar, circled below. To change the text to bold, select the bold icon. For italic text, select the italic icon. For strike text, select the strike icon.

For underlined text, go up to the 'format' menu, then select 'underlined'.

Text Size & Font

To change the size of the font, first select the cells you want to format.

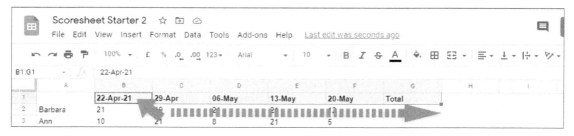

On the toolbar you'll see a font typeface and a font size drop down box. Click on the font size drop down box, then select a size from the list. You can also type in a number to resize the selected text.

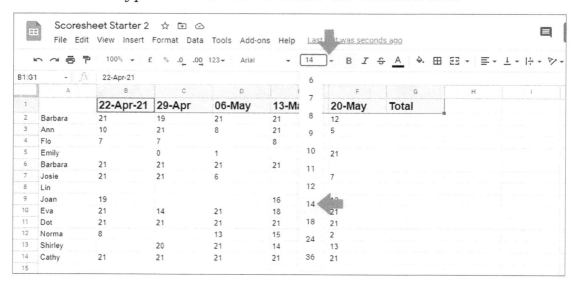

To change the font typeface, click on the font typeface drop down box, then select a font.

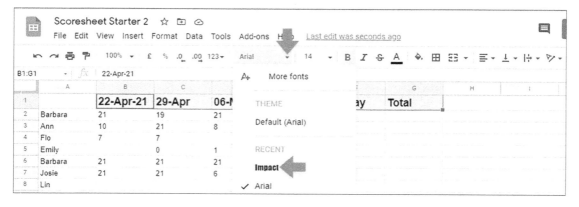

Click on 'more fonts' to see the full list.

Cell Borders

To apply borders to your spreadsheet, select with your mouse the cells you want to format. In this case, I am going to do the whole table.

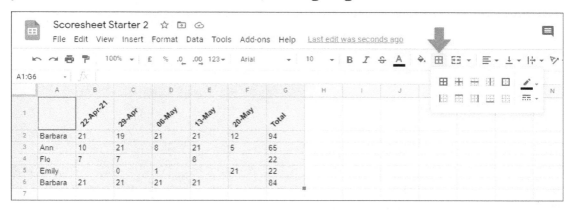

From the toolbar, click on the borders icon. From the drop down menu, select the borders you want to apply from the top row.

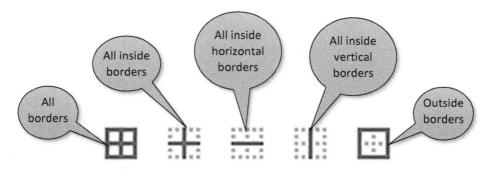

If you select any of the 'Inside borders', this applies the border to the inside of your selection, not the outline, as show below.

	22-Apr-21	29-Apr	06-May	13-May	20-May	Total
Barbara	21	19	21	21	12	94
Ann	10	21	8	21	5	65
Flo	7	7		8		22
Emily		0	1		21	22
Barbara	21	21	21	21		84

'Outside borders' applies the border to the outline of your selection.

	22-Apr-21	29-Apr	06-May	13-May	20-May	Total
Barbara	21	19	21	21	12	94
Ann	10	21	8	21	5	65
Flo	7	7		8		22
Emily		0	1		21	22
Barbara	21	21	21	21		84

Chapter 3: Building Spreadsheets

I want the borders around all the cells both inside and the outline. So from the dialog box click 'all borders'.

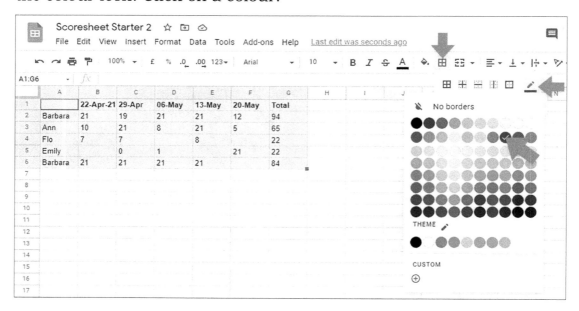

You can also change the colour of the border. To do this, click the borders icon from the toolbar, then from the drop down menu, select the colour icon. Click on a colour.

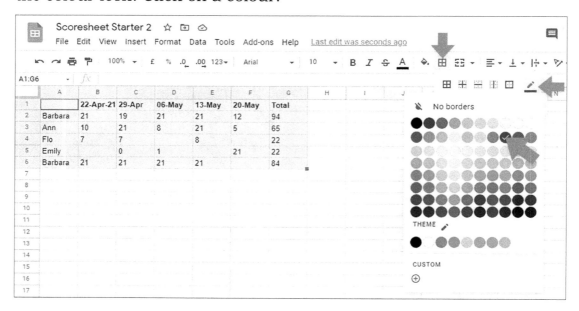

Now, select the border you want to apply such as 'all borders'.

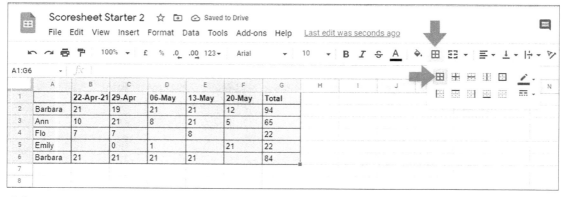

You can change the thickness of the border. To do this, click borders icon from the toolbar, then from the drop down menu, select the border thickness icon. Click on a line thickness.

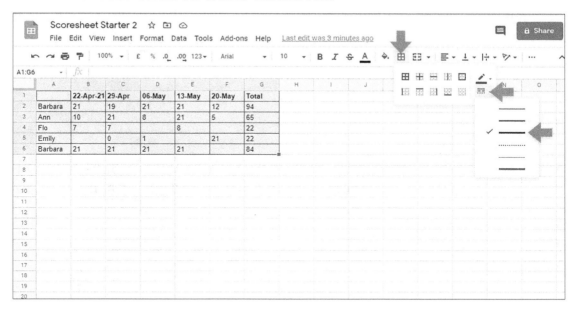

Now, select the border you want to apply such as 'outer borders' to create a bolder outline.

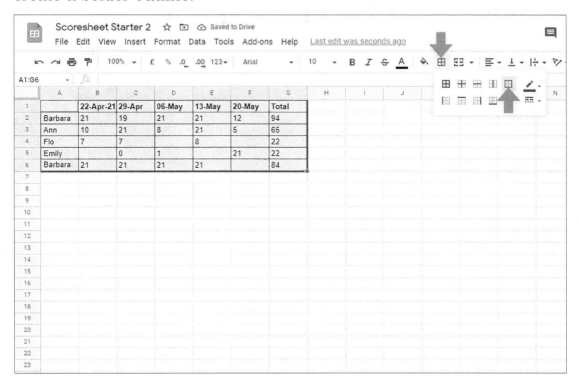

Try some of the other colours and sizes to see how they look

Opening a New Sheet

Within your Google Sheets workbook, you can open more then one spreadsheet. To do this, click the '+' icon on the bottom left of your screen.

You'll see another blank tab appear along the bottom. Double click on the name of the sheet, 'sheet2' in this case, and enter a meaningful name.

Duplicate or Delete a Sheet

To duplicate a sheet, click the small down arrow to the right of the sheet name.

To duplicate the sheet, delete 'duplicate' from the popup menu. Double click on the duplicated sheet's name, then enter a meaningful name.

To delete the sheet, select 'delete'.

Freeze Panes

Large tables or long lists of data can often be difficult to read on a computer screen, sometimes scrolling down the list you can lose track of headings. To combat this, Google Sheets has a feature that allows you to freeze a row or column, meaning the row/column will be on the screen at all times while you scroll down or across your screen. This is called 'freeze panes'.

If we have a look at our distribution list, the list is quite long. It would be far easier to read if we froze the top row.

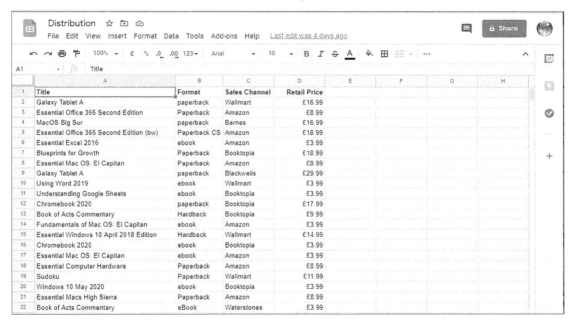

To do this, go to your view menu, go down to 'freeze'. From the slideout menu, select '1 row'. This is the top row of the list containing the headings.

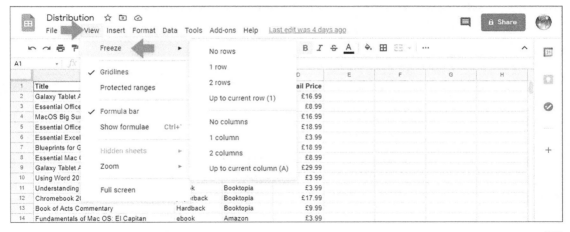

Chapter 3: Building Spreadsheets

Now when you scroll down the list, the top row remains visible.

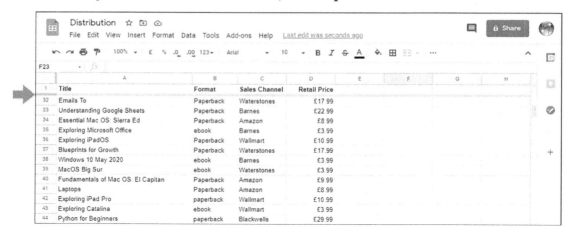

You can do the same with the first column. Click '1 column' instead, from the drop down menu.

In the score sheet example, if I wanted the column with the player names as well as the dates to remain visible, you can do this with freeze panes.

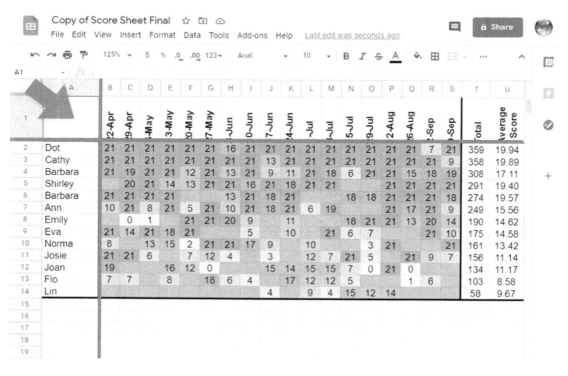

Google Sheets will apply the freeze to the <u>rows below</u> and the <u>columns to the right</u> of the cell you have selected. So in the example above, I have selected the cell A1 because I want to freeze this row (the dates), and column (the names), as you can see in the screen print above.

Once you have selected the cell. From your view menu, go down to 'freeze'.

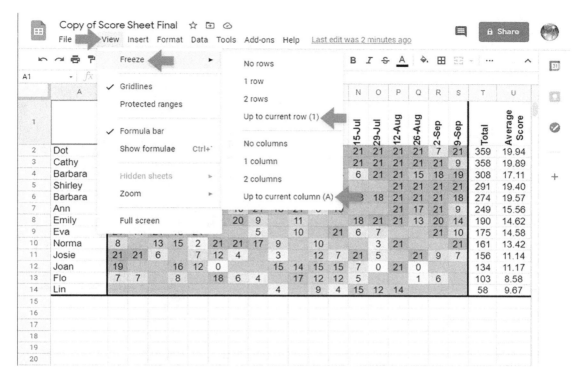

From the slideout menu, select 'up to current row'. Then select 'up to current column.

Try another example... Here, we're freezing up to row 5 and column D.

Conditional Formatting

Conditional formatting allows you to change the format of a cell depending on the cell's contents or value. For example, in our score sheet, I want to highlight all the wins for each player. In this particular sport a score of 21 is a win, so we can apply some conditional formatting to change the colour of each cell with the number 21.

Chapter 3: Building Spreadsheets

First, highlight the range of cells you want to apply the conditional formatting to. In this example, it's the range B2 to S14 - all the player's scores.

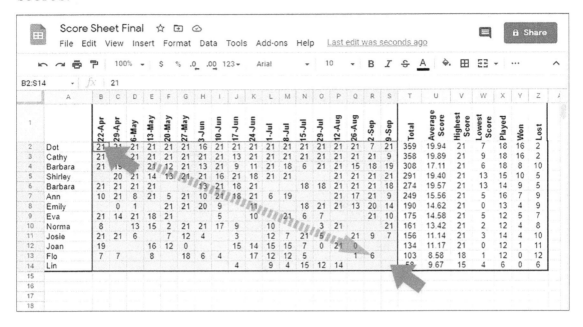

Next, from 'format' menu, select 'conditional formatting'.

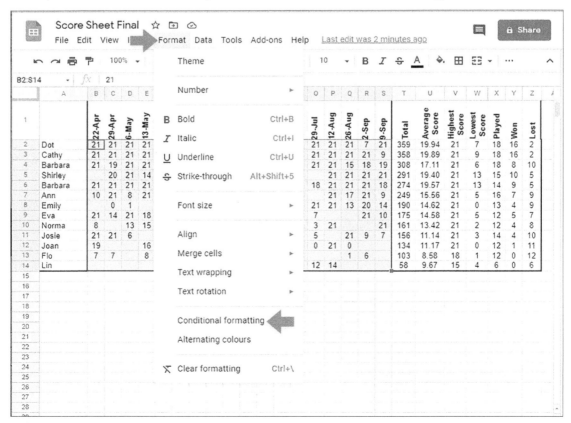

We want to highlight the cells that have a score of 21, so on the sidebar on the right hand side, select the 'single colour' tab.

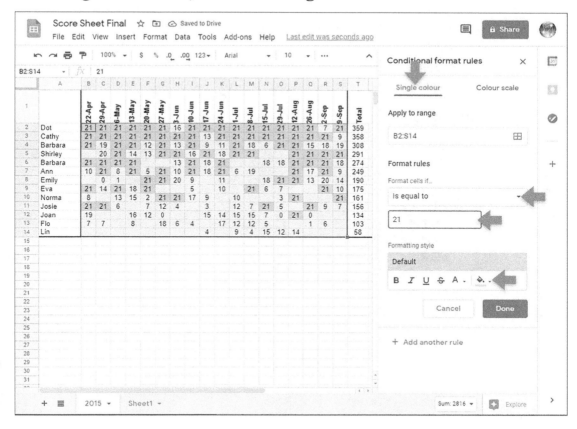

Under 'formatting rules', select your conditions. In this example, we're highlighting cells with a value equal to 21, so select 'is equal to' from the drop down box 'format cells if...' Enter 21 in the value field.

In the 'formatting style' section, select the format you want to apply to the cells. Green is usually good to indicate positives like a win, so click the 'paint pot' icon, then select green. You can also use the other controls to make the text bold, or change the text colour. Click 'done' when you're finished.

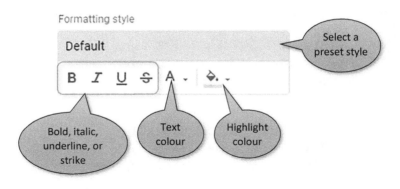

Chapter 3: Building Spreadsheets

Taking it a step further, you can also apply a colour scale effect to the cells according to their value. For example, in our scoring sheet, you could have a different shade for each value. 21 being the highest score and a win could be dark green, and each value below 21 could have a lighter shade as the number decreases. So you end up with a very light green at the lowest scores. You can do this with colour scales. From 'format' menu, select 'conditional formatting'.

From the sidebar that appears on the right, elect 'colour scales'.

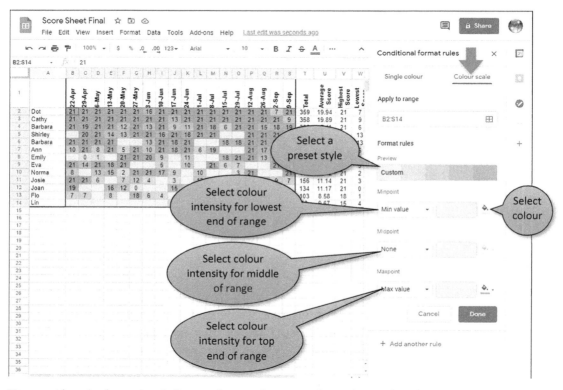

From the 'minpoint' drop down box, select 'number'. In this example, the minimum value would be the lowest score possible which is 0.

So enter '0' into the text box to the right. Click on the 'paint pot' icon then select a colour for the lowest values, eg 'light green'.

From the 'maxpoint' drop down box, select 'number'. In this example, the maximum value would be the highest score possible which is 21.

So enter '21' into the text box to the right. Click on the 'paint pot' icon then select a colour for the highest values, eg 'dark green'.

You should end up with something like this...

	22-Apr	29-Apr	6-May	13-May	20-May	27-May	3-Jun	10-Jun	17-Jun	24-Jun	1-Jul	8-Jul	15-Jul	29-Jul	12-Aug	26-Aug	2-Sep	9-Sep	Total
Dot	21	21	21	21	21	21	16	21	21	21	21	21	21	21	21	21	7	21	359
Cathy	21	21	21	21	21	21	21	21	13	21	21	21	21	21	21	21	21	9	358
Barbara	21	19	21	21	12	21	13	21	9	11	21	18	6	21	21	15	18	19	308
Shirley		20	21	14	13	21	21	16	21	18	21	21			21	21	21	21	291
Barbara	21	21	21	21			13	21	18	21			18	18	21	21	21	18	274
Ann	10	21	8	21	5	21	10	21	18	21	6	19			21	17	21	9	249
Emily		0	1		21	21	20	9		11			18	21	21	13	20	14	190
Eva	21	14	21	18	21			5		10		21	6	7			21	10	175
Norma	8		13	15	2	21	21	17	9		10			3	21			21	161
Josie	21	21	6		7	12	4		3		12	7	21	5		21	9	7	156
Joan	19			16	12	0			15	14	15	15	7	0	21	0			134
Flo	7	7			8		18	6	4		17	12	12	5			1	6	103
Lin									4		9	4	15	12	14				58

As you can see the higher the score, the darker the colour. This is useful for making totals at a glance easier to process.

Formulas and Functions

In this section, we'll take a look at creating formulas to manipulate data and basic functions.

Before we begin, throughout this section, we will be using the resource files. You can download these files from

`videos.tips/functions-googlesheets`

Go down to the files section and click the icons to download the documents to the documents folder on your PC, then import them into google sheets.

Using Formulas

If I wanted to add up all the scores in my score sheet, I could add another column called total and enter a formula to add up the scores for the two weeks the player has played.

To do this, I need to find the cell references for Barbara's scores.

Her scores are in row 2 and columns B and C circled below.

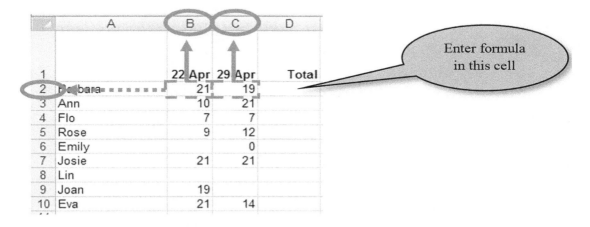

So the cell references are B2 for her score of 21, and C2 for her score of 19.

So we enter into the cell under the heading 'total'

    = B2+C2

Remember all formulas must start with an equals sign **(=)**.

To save you entering the formula for each row, you can replicate it instead.

If you click on the cell D2, where you entered the formula above, you will notice on the bottom right of the box, a small square handle.

I've enlarged the image so you can see it clearly.

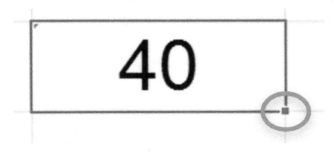

Drag this handle down the rest of the column. You can also double click this handle to fill the rest of the column automatically.

	A	B	C	D	E	F	G
	Player	22-Apr-	29-Apr-	Total			
1	Barbara	21	19	40			
2	Ann	10	21				
3	Flo	7	7				
4	Rose	9	21				
5	Emily		0				
6	Josie	21	21				
7	Lin						
8	Joan	19					
9	Eva	21	14				

Google Sheets will automatically copy the formula and calculate the rest of the totals for you, without you having to enter the formulas for each row.

BIDMAS Rule

BIDMAS (sometimes BODMAS) is an acronym commonly used to remember mathematical operator priority.

Brackets ( )
Indices (square roots: $\sqrt{}$, exponents: squared^2 or cubed^3)
Divide /
Multiply *
Add +
Subtract -

For example, if you wanted to add 20% sales tax to a price of £12.95, you could do something like this...

$$Total = 12.95 + \left(12.95 * \frac{20}{100} \right)$$

Do the bit circled in red first [multiply & divide], then the addition.

Using Functions

A function is a pre-defined formula. Google Sheets has hundreds of different functions all designed to make analysing your data easier. You can find most of these functions under the formulas icon on the toolbar. *If you don't see the functions icon, click the 'three dots' icon on the right of the toolbar.*

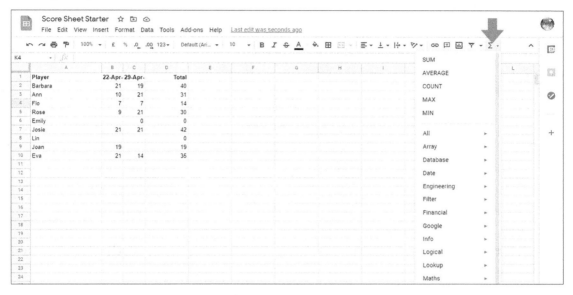

Common functions appear at the top of the list, any other available functions are sorted into groups, just click on these to view the list of functions.

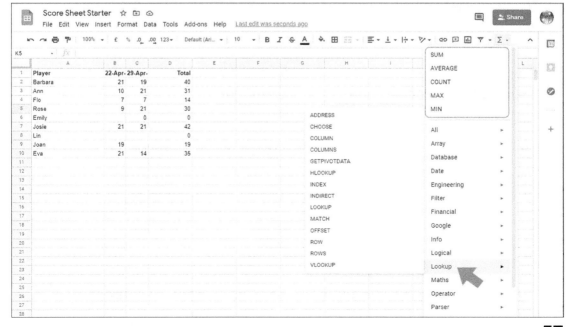

Auto Sum

If I wanted to add a function to cell D2, click on D2, then select the function icon on the toolbar. From the drop down menu, select the function you want. In this example, I want to add up the scores for each player. This is simple addition, so I'd select the 'sum' function.

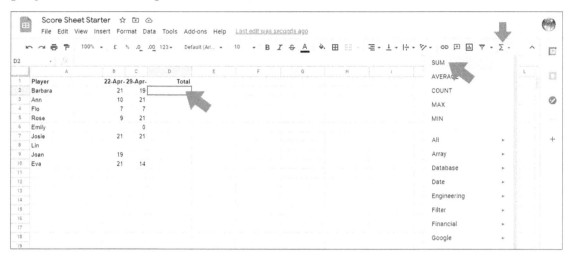

Now select the cells you want to apply the function to. In this case, click on B2 and drag the marker to C2.

Press enter on your keyboard to execute the function.

If you select the cell, you'll see the formula/function appear in the 'fx' bar underneath the toolbar.

Count

Say I wanted to count the number of games played automatically. I could do this with a function.

Insert a new column after "29 Apr" into the spreadsheet and call it "Played". To do this, right click on the D column (the 'Total' column) and from the menu select 'insert 1 left'.

Make sure you have selected the cell you want the formula to appear in, then select the 'function' icon from the toolbar. From the drop down menu, select 'count'.

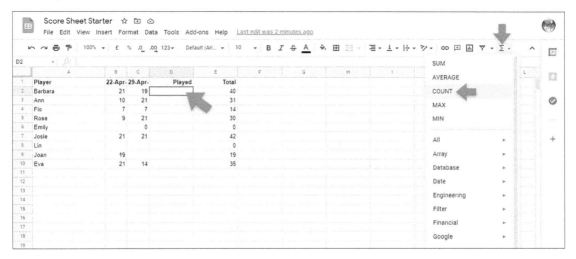

Now we need to tell the count function what we want it to count. We want to count the number of games played. Barbara's scores are in cells B2:S2, so highlight these by dragging your mouse over them, as shown below

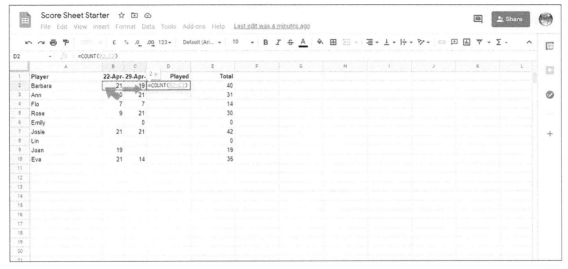

Chapter 4: Formulas and Functions

You can see she has played 2 games. Now we can replicate the formula as we did before. Click and drag the small square handle on the bottom right hand side of the cell.

Drag it down to fill the rest of the column.

CountIf

Counting the number of wins gets a little bit more tricky. In this particular sport, a win is the first to 21 points. So we can count the '21s' in the players' scores. To do this, we use the 'CountIf' function. This function counts a value depending on a certain condition, in this case if the value is 21 or not.

I have inserted another column called 'wins'. Click in the first cell of that column. This is where we want the result to appear.

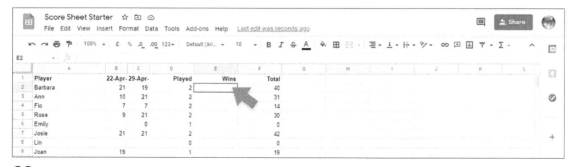

Select the 'function' icon from the toolbar. You'll find this function in the 'maths' category in the drop down menu. From the slide out menu, select 'countif'.

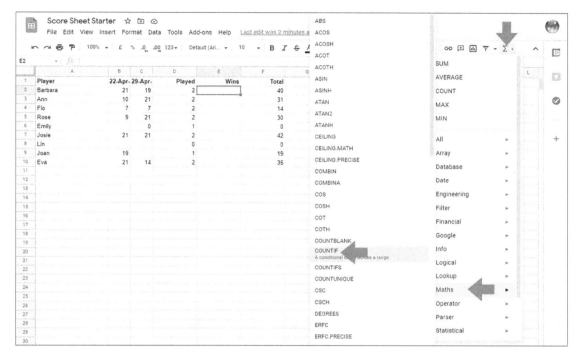

Select the cells you want to count. Eg click and drag the cells B2 to C2.

This particular function requires two parameters - the range selected above, and a condition. Parameters must be separated by a comma.

```
countif (range, condition)
```

The condition in this case is 21 as we want to count all the cells containing the number 21. So we enter a comma (after the range), followed by the number 21.

Average

Average finds the middle number in a row or column. To find the average, click on the cell you want the result to appear in. In this example, I have inserted a column for average score, and I want the average for the first player to appear in cell U2, shown below in the illustration.

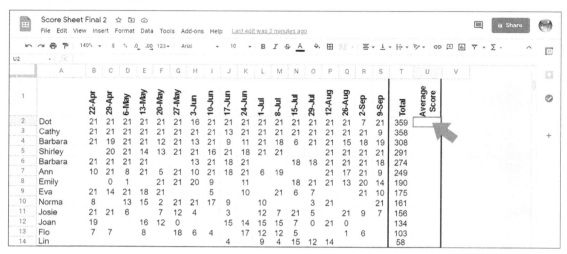

We'll need to add the average function. To do this, click on the 'function' icon on the toolbar. Select 'average' from the drop down menu. If you don't see the average function, you'll find it in the 'statistical' section of the menu.

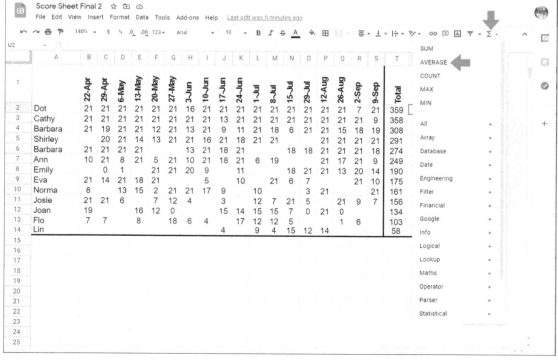

Select the cells you want to average. To do this, click on the cell B2 and drag the box across to S2. Press enter on your keyboard to execute the function.

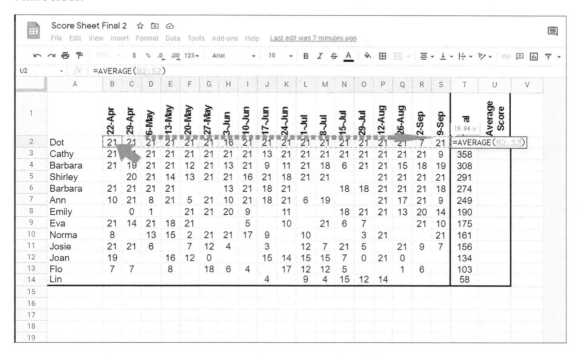

Now replicate the function down the rest of the column.

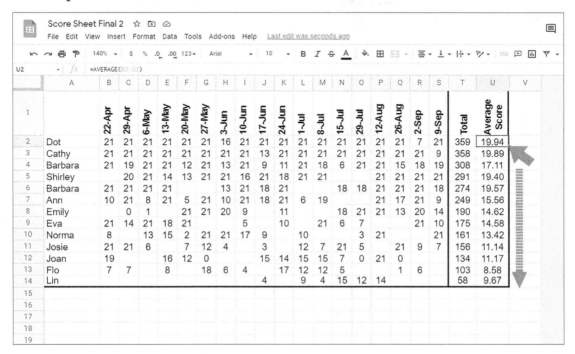

Drag it down to fill the rest of the column as shown above.

Max & Min

Max returns the largest number in a selected range of values, and min returns the smallest number.

Select the cell you want the result to appear in. I have added two new columns, one for highest score and one for lowest score. I'm going to use the max function in the 'highest score' column.

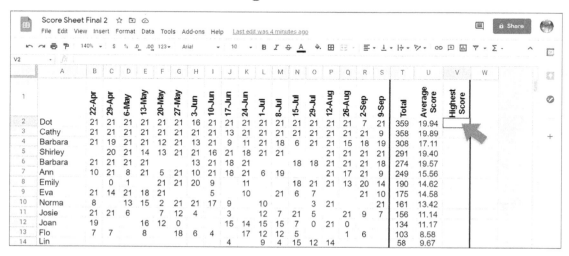

Click on the 'function' icon on the toolbar. Select 'max' from the drop down menu. If you don't see the average function, you'll find it in the 'statistical' section of the menu.

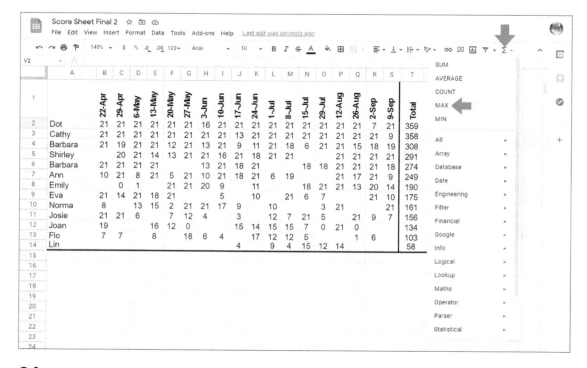

Select the range B2:S2 - click on the cell B2, then drag your mouse pointer over to S2.

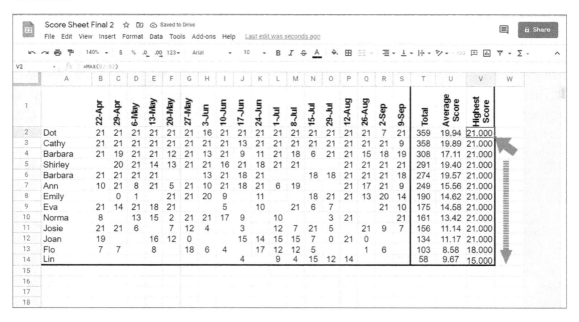

Hit enter to execute the function, then drag the square handle on the bottom right of the cell to replicate the function down the rest of the column.

The procedure is exactly the same for the Min function, except from the auto sum drop down menu select 'min' instead of 'max'.

Give it a try.

IF Function

'If functions' are called conditional functions and test whether a condition is true or false. The function returns a different result for the true condition and another result for false.

```
= (IF condition, result-if-true, result-if-false)
```

Can be read as

```
If test condition is true,
      execute result-if-true
else
      execute result-if-false
```

In this demo, we are going to apply a conditional function to calculate our shipping cost. The rule is, free delivery for orders over £25, otherwise a shipping charge of £3.99 applies.

To insert an IF function, click on the cell you want the calculation to appear in (D12). Then click on the 'function' icon on the toolbar. On the drop down menu, go down to 'logical', then select 'if'.

First, we need to find out if the total is greater than or equal to 25. To do this, select the cell the total is in. The net total is in cell D11, so click D11.

Now, we need to enter the condition. We want to check to see if the total is greater than 25, so type in

```
>= 25
```

Next, we need to tell the IF function what to do if the value is over 25 (ie true). In this case we want to return 0 for free shipping.

```
>= 25, 0
```

Finally, we need to tell the IF function what to do if the value is not over 25 (ie false). In this case we want to return 3.99.

```
>= 25, 0, 3.99
```

You should end up with something like this.

```
= IF (D11 >= 25, 0, 3.99)
```

Because the net total is £27.46, this is over 25, so the shipping is 0.

Try adjusting the number of items and see what happens when the total goes below £25.

VLookup

VLOOKUP searches for a value in the first column of a specified table, and returns a value from the specified adjacent column.

```
=VLOOKUP (value to look for,
          table to retrieve value from,
               column number with value to return,
                    true for exact/false for approx)
```

In the example, we are going to apply a lookup function to calculate our shipping cost according to the shipping rates table (F15:G20).

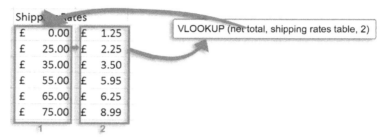

To insert a VLOOKUP, click on the cell you want the calculation to appear in (D12), then click on the 'function' icon on the toolbar.

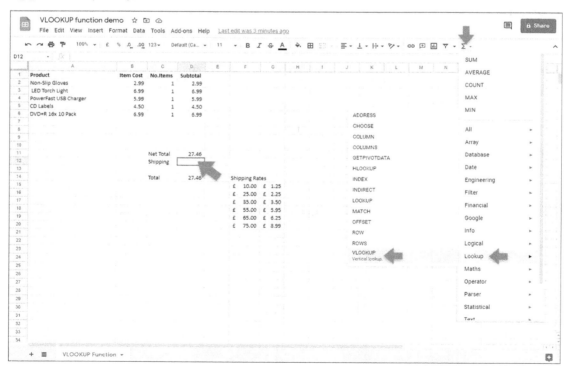

From the drop down menu, go down to 'lookup', then select 'vlookup' from the slideout menu.

First we need to enter the lookup value. This is the value we want to look up in the shipping rates table. In this case the net total is in cell D11, so click D11 to add the cell to the 'lookup value' field. After you've selected the cell, enter a comma.

D12		fx	=VLOOKUP(D11)					
	A	B	C	D	E	F	G	H
1	Product	Item Cost	No.Items	Subtotal				
2	Non-Slip Gloves	2.99	1	2.99				
3	LED Torch Light	6.99	1	6.99				
4	PowerFast USB Charger	5.99	1	5.99				
5	CD Labels	4.50	1	4.50				
6	DVD+R 16x 10 Pack	6.99	1	6.99				
7								
8								
9								
10								
11			Net Total	27.46				
12			Shipping	=VLOOKUP(D11				
13								
14			Total	27.46		Shipping Rates		
15						£ 10.00	£ 1.25	
16						£ 25.00	£ 2.25	
17						£ 35.00	£ 3.50	
18						£ 55.00	£ 5.95	
19						£ 65.00	£ 6.25	
20						£ 75.00	£ 8.99	
21								

Next click in the 'table array' field. In this field, we want to specify the table of values we are looking up. In this case the table array is the shipping rates table (highlighted in red below). So click on F15 and drag your mouse over to G20, to select the table.

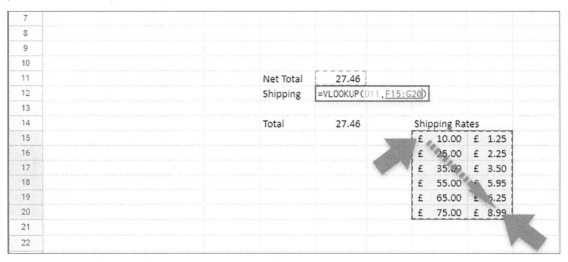

After you've done that, enter another comma.

Next, we need to enter a column index. This is the column in the table that contains the values we want to return. So for example, looking at the shipping rates table, if the net total is under 25, we return 1.25. If the net total is between 25 and 34, we return 2.25 and so on.

The net total range is in column 1 and the shipping rates are in column 2. We want to return the shipping rates in column 2, so type in 2.

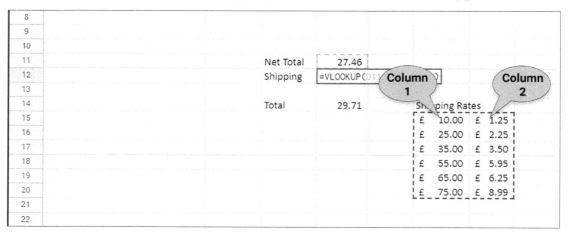

Press enter when you're done.

	A	B	C	D	E	F	G	H
1	Product	Item Cost	No.Items	Subtotal				
2	Non-Slip Gloves	2.99	1	2.99				
3	LED Torch Light	6.99	3	20.97				
4	PowerFast USB Charger	5.99	1	5.99				
5	CD Labels	4.50	1	4.50				
6	DVD+R 16x 10 Pack	6.99	1	6.99				

C3   *fx*   3

Net Total   41.44
Shipping   £   3.50

Total   44.94

Shipping Rates
£   10.00   £   1.25
£   25.00   £   2.25
£   35.00   £   3.50
£   55.00   £   5.95
£   65.00   £   6.25
£   75.00   £   8.99

Try adjusting the item prices or number of items and see what happens to the shipping rate.

Types of Data

There are several different types of data you will come across while using Google Sheets. These data can be numeric such as whole numbers called integers (eg 10), numbers with decimal points (eg 29.93), currencies (eg £4.67 or $43.76), as well as date and time, text and so on.

Going back to our scoring spreadsheet, we need another column for the average scores. Insert a new column and type the heading 'Average' as shown below.

We are going to work out the average scores over the number of games the players have played. In the Cell F2 enter the formula

```
Average = Total Score / Total number of Games Played
```

The total score is in E2 and the total number of games played is in D2.

So we enter into F2:

```
= E2 / D2
```

Use the forward slash for divide: **/**

Replicate the formula down the column as we did previously in the exercise.

Now the number format isn't as accurate as we want it. We need to tell Google Sheets that the data in this column is a number, accurate to two decimal places.

Chapter 4: Formulas and Functions

To do this, highlight the cells you want to apply the number format to, as shown below.

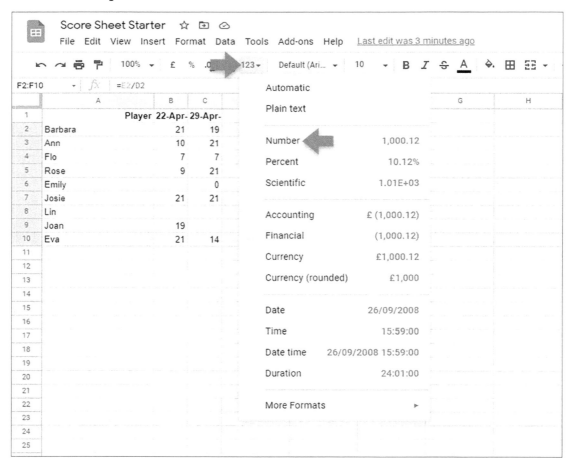

On the toolbar, click on the 'more formats' icon, then select 'number' from the drop down menu.

It would be the same for recording the fees paid by the players. Insert another column and call it 'fee'. Say the fees are 4.50. When we enter 4.5 into the cell, Google Sheets thinks it's just a number, so we need to tell Google Sheets that it is currency.

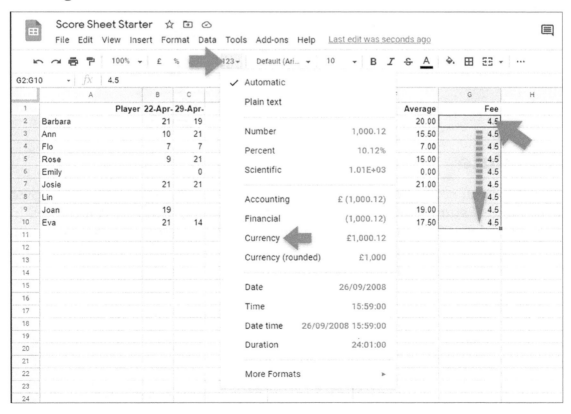

Select all the data in the fee column. You don't need to include the heading row.

From the drop down menu click currency. This will format all the numbers as a currency.

Cell Referencing

In Google Sheets, there are two types of cell referencing to think about when copying formulas to other parts of your spreadsheet. Do you want the formula to reference the same cells regardless of where you paste it? Or do you want the cells referenced in the copied formula, to change relative to their new position? You might use absolute cell referencing when referencing a look up table of values, and relative referencing when you want to total up a column or row.

Relative

Relative cell referencing means that as a formula or function is copied and pasted somewhere else in your spreadsheet, the cell references in the formula or function change to reflect the function's new location.

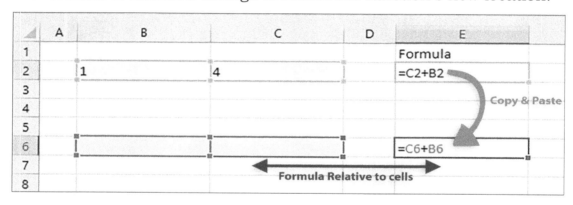

Absolute

Absolute cell referencing means that as a formula or function is copied and pasted somewhere else in your spreadsheet, the cell references in the formula or function do not change, they stay fixed on a specific cell.

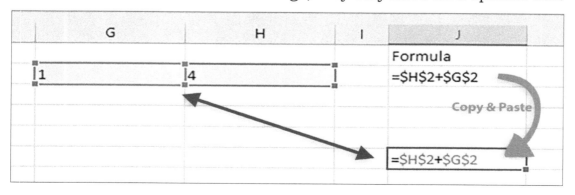

You indicate an absolute cell reference using a dollar sign ($).

Where you put the dollar sign will indicate which row or column is to remain absolute - meaning it doesn't change when you copy the formula.

A1	Column & Row do not change when formula is copied to another cell
A$1	Row does not change, but column will change when formula is copied
$A1	Column does not change, but row will change when formula is copied

All you need to remember is to put the dollar sign before the row or column reference you want to remain the same regardless of where you copy and paste the formula.

Adding Charts

In this section, we'll take a look at creating charts from our data.

Before we begin, throughout this section, we will be using the resource files.

You can download these files from the following website.

`videos.tips/charts-googlesheets`

Go down to the files section and click the icons to download the files to the documents folder on your PC.

Types of Chart

There are many different types of charts to choose from, here are a few examples of some common ones.

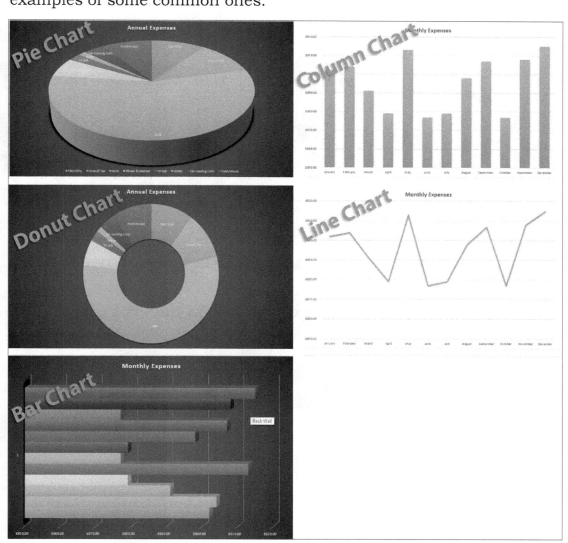

Column and bar charts compare values with each other, line charts show trends over time, donut and pie charts represent proportions of a whole or a percentage.

You will need to use the correct chart for the data you want to represent.

The easiest way to add a chart is to select from your spreadsheet, a column you want for the X-Axis and a column you want for the Y-Axis.

I am going to make a chart on the total scores.

Creating a Chart

First select all the names in the first column. This will be the X-Axis on the chart.

	A	B	C	D	E	F	G
1		22-Apr	29-Apr	Played		Total	Average	Fee
2	Barbara	21	19	2		40	20.00	£9.00
3	Ann	10	21	2		31	15.50	£9.00
4	Flo	7	7	2		14	7.00	£9.00
5	Rose	9	12	2		21	10.50	£9.00
6	Emily		0	1		0	0.00	£9.00
7	Josie	21	21	2		42	21.00	£9.00
8	Lin			0		0	#DIV/0!	£9.00
9	Joan	19		1		19	19.00	£9.00
10	Eva	21	14	2		35	17.50	£9.00
11								

Now hold down the control key (ctrl) on your keyboard. This allows you to multi-select.

While holding down control, select the data in the total column with your mouse.

This will be the Y-Axis on the chart. Note the data in the names column is still highlighted.

E1				f_x	Total			

	A	B	C	D	E	F	G
1		22-Apr	29-Apr	Played		Total	Average	Fee
2	Barbara	21	19	2		40	20.00	£9.00
3	Ann	10	21	2		31	15.50	£9.00
4	Flo	7	7	2		14	7.00	£9.00
5	Rose	9	12	2		21	10.50	£9.00
6	Emily		0	1		0	0.00	£9.00
7	Josie	21	21	2		42	21.00	£9.00
8	Lin			0		0	#DIV/0!	£9.00
9	Joan	19		1		19	19.00	£9.00
10	Eva	21	14	2		35	17.50	£9.00

Release the control key.

Go to the 'insert' menu and select 'chart'. You'll see a default chart appear under your spreadsheet and a 'chart editor' panel open up on the right hand side.

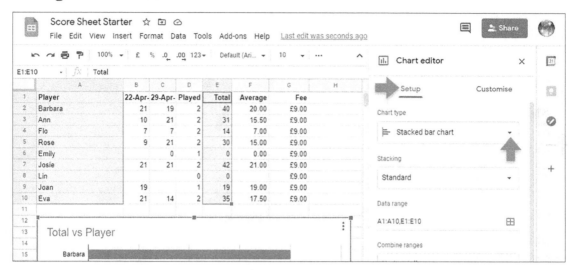

I am going for a column chart. To do this, select the 'setup' tab in the 'chart editor' panel, then under chart type select 'column chart'.

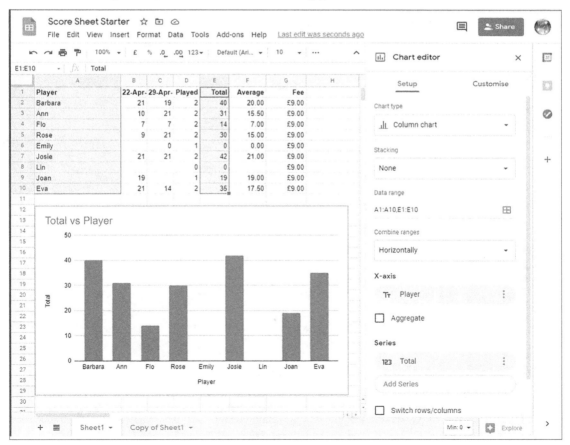

Chapter 5: Adding Charts

You can also change the data range if you need to, eg select a different column. To do this, under the 'data range' section, click on the grid icon.

Select the cells you want to include in your chart. Eg if I wanted the average score instead of the total (on the y axis). I'd change the data range in the second range from E1:E10 to F1:F10 as shown below.

If you need to add another column or data range, click 'add another range', then select the cells you want to add.

If you want to add another series to show on the chart, then click on 'add series', then select the grid icon.

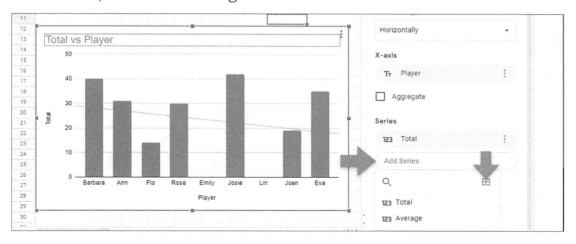

Select the cells you want to add. In this example, I'm going to add the average score as another column.

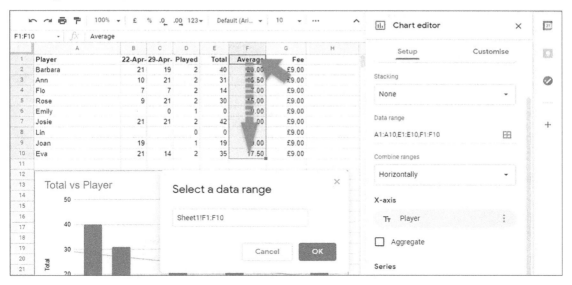

Click 'ok'. You can see the average score appears as another column.

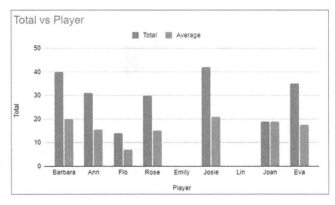

Formatting Charts

You can format and customise the individual chart elements, such as the axis, axis titles, chart title, data labels, gridlines and the legend. To do this, select the 'customise' tab in the 'chart editor' panel on the right hand side.

Chart Style

From the chart style section, you can change the background colour, font, chart border and add a 3D effect.

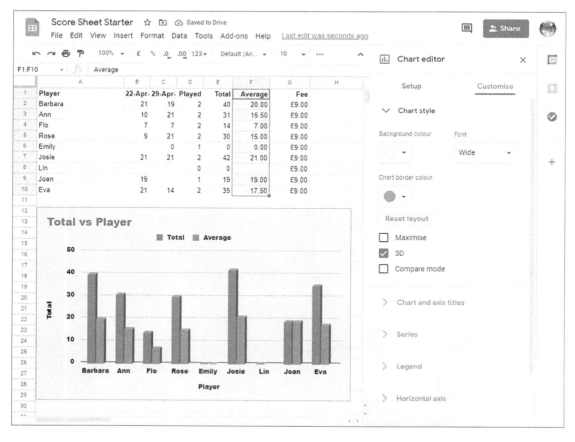

Compare mode is useful for line charts and provides additional information when we hover over a data value with your mouse.

Chart and Axis Titles

On some charts, Google Sheets might not have added any axis titles. If this is the case, you can change the titles using the 'chart and axis titles' section in the chart editor.

To change the text in the axis titles, click on the 'chart title' drop down box. Select 'chart title' to change the chart title, select 'chart subtitle' to add or change the subtitle, select 'horizontal axis title' or 'vertical axis title' to change the axis titles.

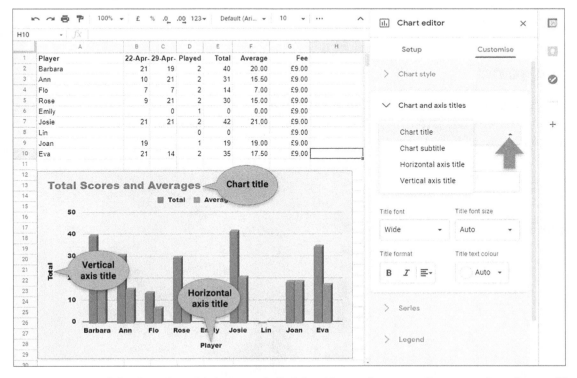

Type your title in the 'title text' field. Also change font and colour if needed using the 'title font' and size fields underneath.

Series

From the series section, you can change the data series for the x axis or the y axis.

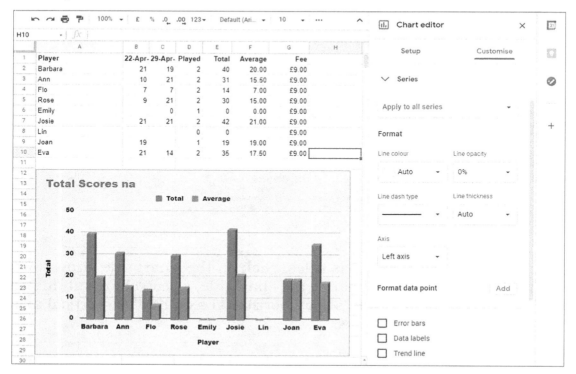

Legend

Here you can customise the chart legend, ie the key descriptions of the data entries on the chart. In this example the legend is shown at the top of the chart: 'total' and 'average'.

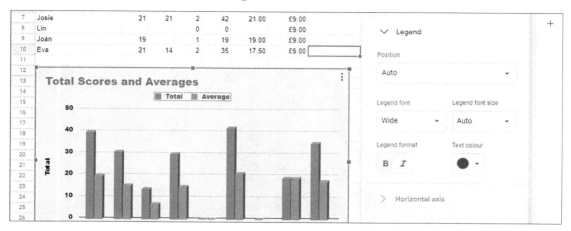

You can change the position, the legend font, text colour and size.

Horizontal & Vertical Axis

In this section, you can customise the chart axis. You can change the font, size and colour, as well as slant the labels as shown below to make reading your chart clearer.

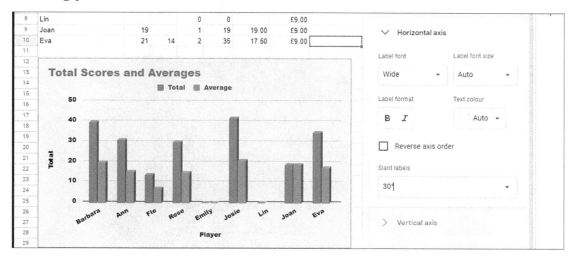

Gridlines and Ticks

Here, you can adjust the scales on the axis. Use the top drop down box to select which axis you want to adjust.

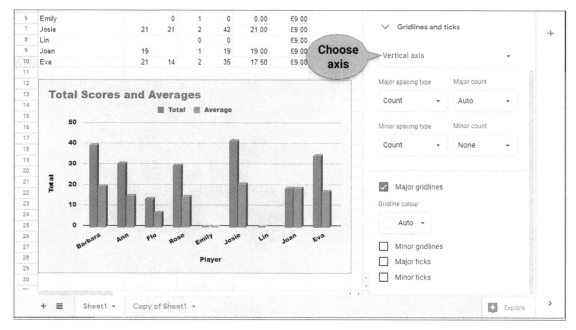

Using the settings underneath, you can change the spacing, scale/count, gridlines and grid colour.

Move and Resize Charts

To resize, click on a blank section of your chart. You'll notice some small white dots appear around the chart. These are called resize handles.

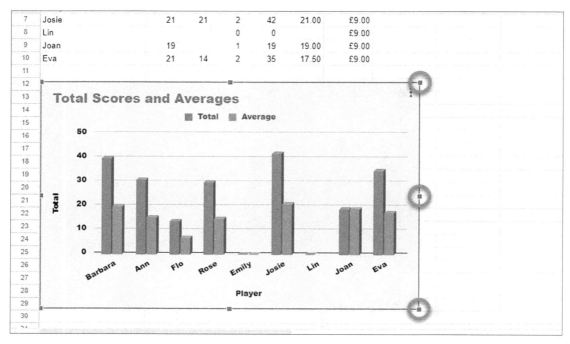

Drag the resize handles across your page to the size you want the chart.

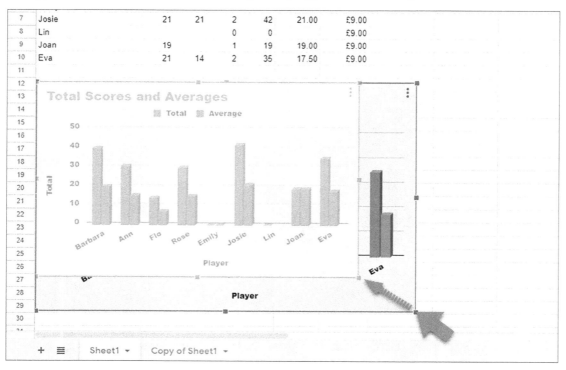

To move your chart into position, click in a blank section of your chart, then drag it with your mouse into a new position.

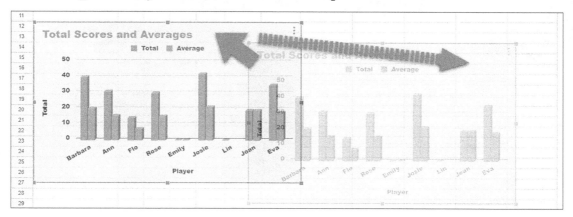

More Options

When you click on your chart, you'll see a 'three dots' icon on the top right. Click on this icon to reveal the 'more options' menu.

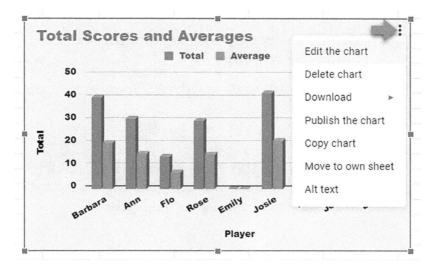

Here you can edit your chart - this opens the chart editor, or you can delete your chart.

You can download your chart as a PNG, PDF, or SVG file which can be used to paste into another software application or published on a web page.

You can publish the chart and create a link to send to other people.

You can also copy the chart or move the chart to it's own sheet.

Finally you can add 'alt text', which is useful for when publishing the chart as a PNG on a website.

Data Analysis

In this section, we'll take a look analysing our data with goal seek, scenario manager, slicers, and pivot tables.

Before we begin, throughout this section, we will be using the resource files.

You can download these files from the following website.

`videos.tips/data-googlesheets`

Go down to the files section and click the icons to download the files to the documents folder on your PC then import them into google sheets..

Goal Seek

Goal seek allows you start with the desired result, the goal in other words, and calculates the value required to give you that result.

For this example, use the **goal seek** worksheet in the **Data Analysis Starter.xlsx** workbook.

To use goal seek, first you'll need to download the addon. To do this, go to the 'add-ons' menu, then select 'get addons'.

In the search field at the top of the window, type in goal seek. Click on the addon in the search results.

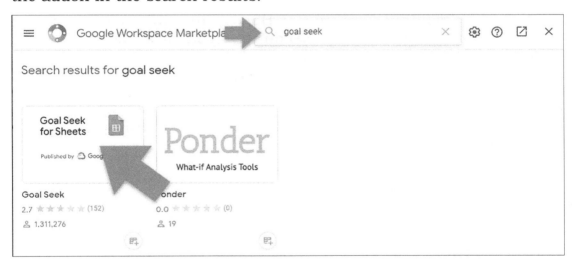

Click 'install' to add the addon to Google Sheets.

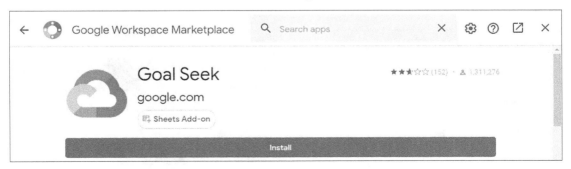

Click on your google account, sign in if you're prompted, then select 'allow'.

Chapter 6: Data Analysis

Say we want to take out a loan of £10,000. This particular bank has an interest rate of 3.3%. We're paying the loan off over 60 months with a payment of £181.02. We can afford to pay off £200 per month. We can use goal seek to find out how many months we'll be paying the loan off.

From the 'addon' menu, go down to 'goal seek'. From the slideout down select, click 'open'. You'll see a panel open on the right hand side.

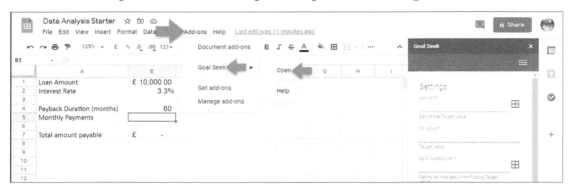

First click the monthly payment (cell B5), because this is what we want to change. On the 'goal seek' panel on the right, click the 'capture cell' icon next to the first field 'set cell'.

In the next field 'to value', and enter 200. This is our target amount or goal.

Now we want to achieve this goal by changing the payback duration, so click in cell B4, the cell with the number of months.

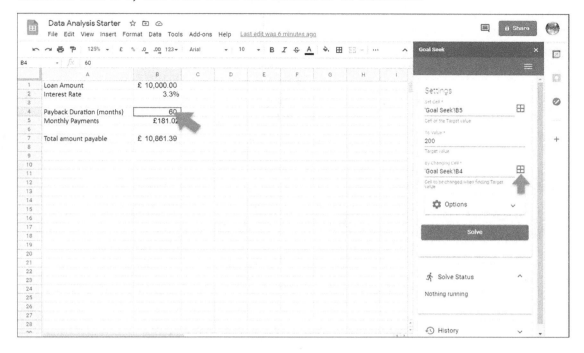

Click 'solve'. We have an answer... It would take 54 months at £200 a month.

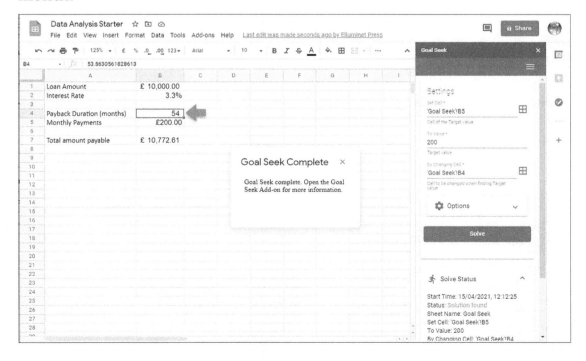

Creating Pivot Tables

A pivot table is a data summarisation tool and can automatically sort, count, total or average the data stored in one table or worksheet and display the results in a new table or worksheet. Reports can then be produced to present the data.

With a pivot table you can quickly pivot data, meaning you reorganise or summarise the data. Pivoting data can help you answer different scenarios, for example, best selling products, sales channels and so on.

For this example, use the **pivot table data** worksheet in the **Data Analysis Starter.xlsx** workbook. Import the file into Google Sheets.

First click in any cell in the data table. This is to indicate to Google Sheets what table of data it should use to create the pivot table. From the 'data' menu, select 'pivot table'.

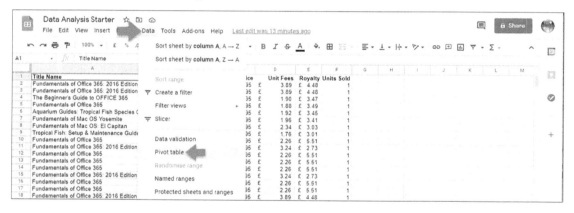

Make sure Google Sheets has selected the correct range in the 'select a table or range' field. Click 'create' on the popup dialog box.

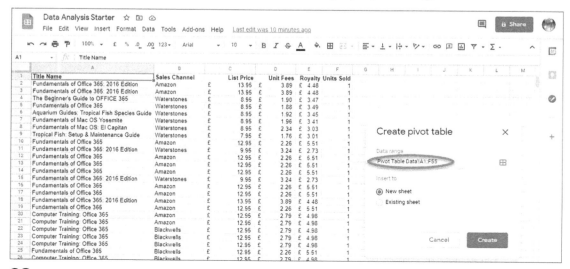

You'll see your 'PivotTable Editor' sidebar open on the right hand side. From here we can start building pivot tables.

Here, you can add and remove fields.

Any field you add to the rows section will appear down the left hand side of the table and anything you drag to the columns section will appear as columns across the top of your table. This makes up the row and column headers of the pivot table.

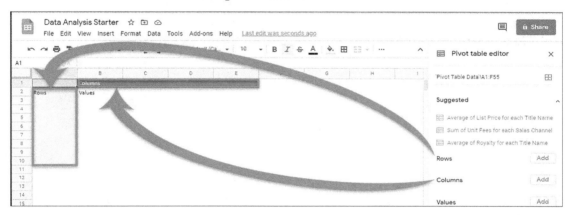

So next to 'rows', click 'add'. We want to use add 'title name'. To add the columns, click 'add' next to 'columns' and select 'sales channels'.

The values section, is the data you want to analyse against the rows and column headers.

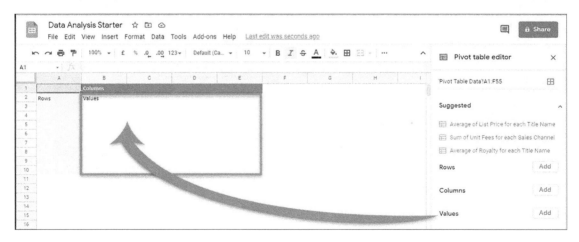

In the values section, we could add the 'royalty' field to see how much income is generated for each title in each sales channel. Or we could add 'units sold' to the values section to see how many books have sold in each sales channel.

Click 'add' next to the 'values' section, then select 'royalty'.

Chapter 6: Data Analysis

This is what we'll end up with. We have all the book titles against the sales channels.

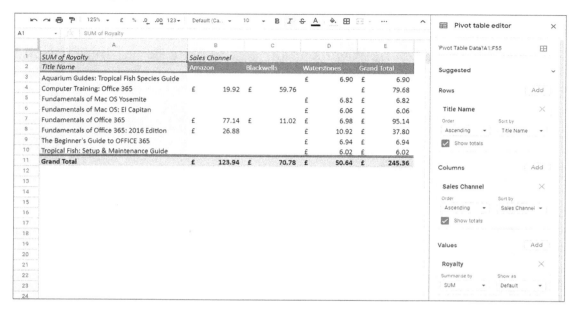

You'll also see the values are the royalties earned for each book title in the sales channels - Amazon, Blackwells and Waterstones, as well as grand totals. In this case Amazon generated the highest revenue (£123.94).

How about the number of books sold? We can answer this question by adding the 'units sold' field.

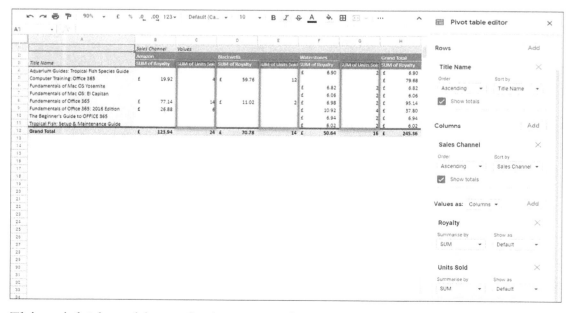

This might be a bit confusing to read. To make the data analysis easier, Google Sheets has a feature called slicers.

Using Slicers

A slicer is essentially a filter, and allows you to filter the data in the pivot table to make things easier to analyse.

In the above example, we can see both units sold and the royalties for each sales channel, all on one table. To make things easier to analyse, we can add a slicer for sales channels that will enable us to select a sales channel, and display a pivot table for only that channel.

This helps break your data down into more concise parts.

To insert a slicer, go to the 'data' menu and select 'slicer'.

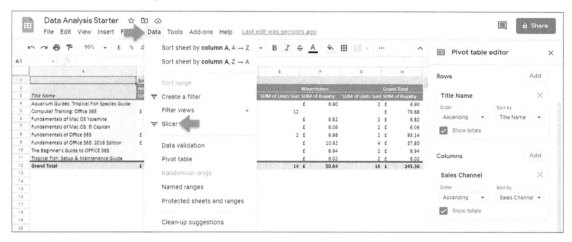

From the 'insert slicers' panel that opens up, click the field you want to organise the data by. In this example we are organising the data by sales channel, so click 'sales channel'.

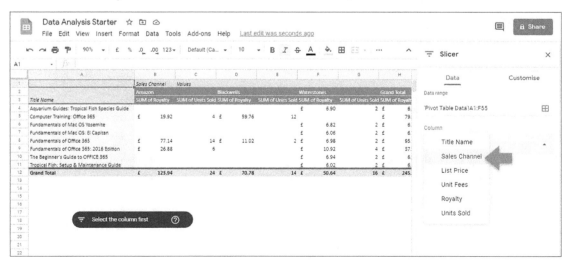

You'll see a slicer pop up underneath your pivot table.

Chapter 6: Data Analysis

Select the sales channels you want to show. If you select 'amazon' you'll see all sales, etc from the amazon channel. Similarly if you select 'blackwells' or 'waterstones' you'll see sales from those channels.

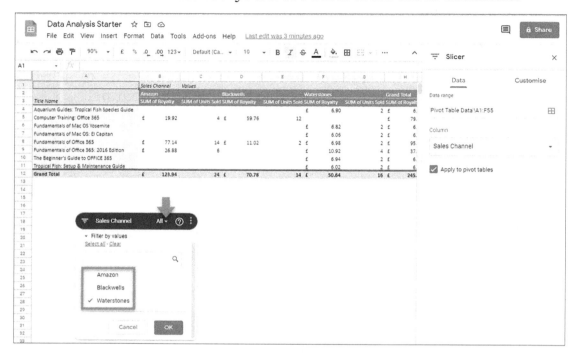

Click 'ok'.

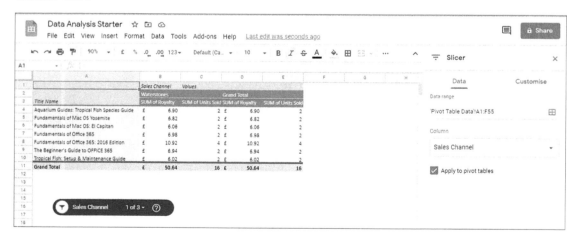

Here, you'll see the data for your slicer. Double click on your slicer to open up the 'slicer' side panel where you can change the data range and customise the font, size, colour, etc.

Sorting Pivot Table Data

You can also sort data in these tables in the same way you'd sort any column in your spreadsheet.

Say we wanted to find the best selling book?

I can adjust my pivot table to show total books sold (just need 'title name' and 'units sold' fields).

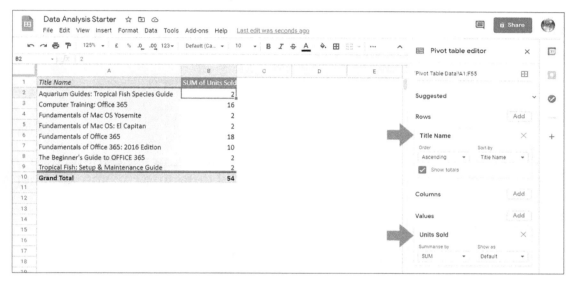

To sort the data, click on a cell in your pivot table, then use the 'sort by' field in the rows section of the 'pivot table editor' panel on the right.

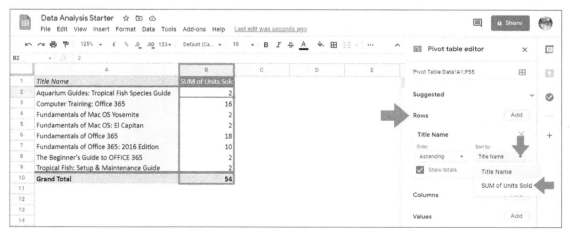

Set the 'sort by' field to 'SUM of Units Sold' - ie total number of books sold column in our pivot table.

Next set 'order' to 'descending' - as we want the largest number of sales to show first.

Data Validation

In this section, we'll take a look data validation rules to make sure users enter valid data into the spreadsheet.

Before we begin, throughout this section, we will be using the resource files.

You can download these files from

`videos.tips/validation-googlesheets`

Go down to the files section and click the icons to download the files to the documents folder on your PC, then import them into google sheets.

Validation Rules

In Google Sheets, you can set a variety of rules to cells to help users enter the correct data.

Lets take a look at an example in the **Data Validation Demo.xlsx** workbook.

By Data Type

Whole numbers are called integers in Google Sheets and do not have any decimal places. In the example, we can add a validation check to the 'number of items' column. It's safe to assume that these will only be whole numbers, don't think anyone will try order half an LED torch light.

Select the cells to apply the validation check to.

	A	B	C	D	E	F	G	H
1	SKU	Product	Item Cost	No.Items	Subtotal			
2	11255	Non-Slip Gloves	2.99	4	11.96			
3	11467	LED Torch Light	6.99	1	6.99			
4	11477	PowerFast USB Charger	5.99	1	5.99			
5	11576	CD Labels	4.50	9	42.30			
6	11554	DVD+R 16x 10 Pack	6.99	3	20.97			
7								
8								
9				Net Total	88.21			
10				Shipping Method	Standard			
11				Shipping Cost	2.99			
12				Total	91.20			
13								
14								

From the 'data' menu select 'data validation'.

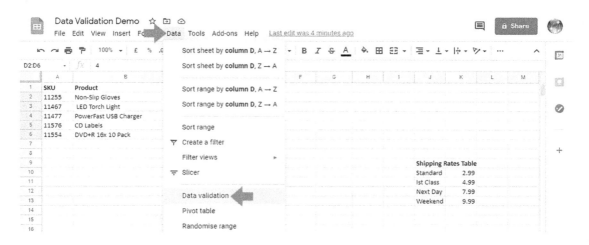

Chapter 7: Data Validation

From the data validation box, click the first drop down box next to 'criteria' and select 'number' - because we only want to allow whole numbers in these cells.

You can also set a criteria for the whole numbers. For example, we could set a range 1 - 500. We could argue that you can't order 0 items on the order form and set a maximum limit of only shipping 500 at a time. So in the data field, select 'between'. Set the minimum value to 1 and the max value to 500.

If there was no maximum limit to the number of items ordered. Instead of selecting 'between' in the data field, you could select 'greater than or equal to' and set the minimum value to 1. Select the middle drop down box and change it to 'greater than'.

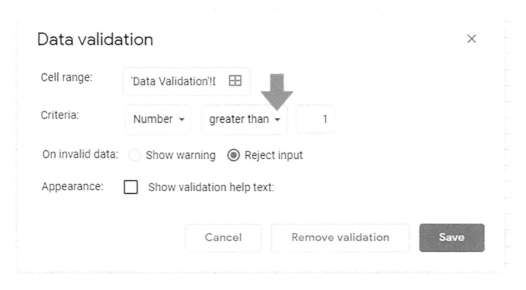

Using the 'on valid data' section, you can choose what to do when a user enters invalid data.

If you select 'show warning', the user will get a warning next to an invalid entry. However, google sheets will allow the entry to remain.

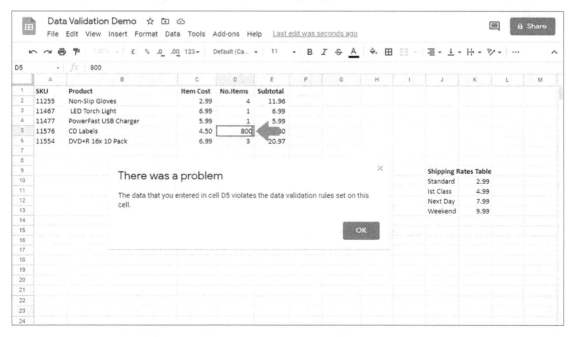

If you select 'reject input', google sheets will ignore any invalid data the user enters and display an error message.

Click 'save' on the 'data validation' window when you're done.

Chapter 7: Data Validation

Text Length

You can enforce a specific length of text or numbers with data validation. In our example, we have a field called SKU, this is a unique product code each product in our catalogue has to identify it. In this case, each SKU is exactly 5 digits long and can't be more than 5 or less than 5 digits.

Select the cells you want to apply the validation to, in this example, it's the SKU column. From the 'data' menu, select 'data validation'.

To enforce our validation rule, we'll need to use a function called LEN. To enter this function, in the 'criteria' section, change the first drop down box to 'custom formula is'.

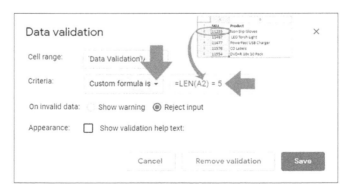

In the next field, enter the following:

```
=LEN(A2) = 5
```

The LEN function takes a cell or string and returns the number of characters. In this case enter the first cell reference in the range: A2. The data validation rules will be added to all the selected cells.

We want the number of characters to be 5 only so we add '= 5'.

Create a Drop Down List

Drop down lists allow the user to select pre-set options allocated to a particular cell, instead of having to type the data in.

If we take a look at an example in the **Data Validation Demo.xlsx** workbook

To create a drop down list, select the cell you want the drop down list to appear in. From the 'data' menu, select 'Data Validation'.

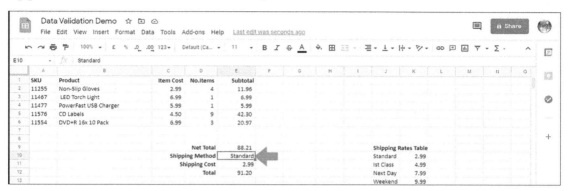

From the dialog box that appears, in the 'criteria' field, click in the drop down, then from the options select 'list from range'.

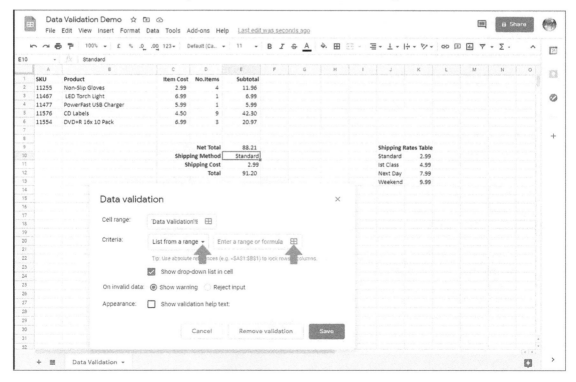

Click the 'range capture' icon to the right of the range field.

Chapter 7: Data Validation

Select the range of values that you want the user to be able to choose from, in the drop down box we're creating. Since we want to create a drop down box for the user to select the shipping rates, we select the shipping from the rates table as shown below.

Click 'ok' when you're done. Click 'save' in the 'data validation' dialog box.

You'll notice a little down arrow appear next to the cell we selected. Click the arrow to select the desired option and see what happens.

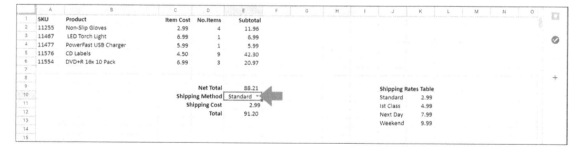

The user will now be able to select the shipping rate.

Locking Cells

When your users are using your spreadsheet, they may accidentally wipe out formulas and cells you don't really want them to change.

Google Sheets allows you to lock cells and cell ranges so your users can't change the contents.

If we take a look at an example in the **Data Validation Demo.xlsx** workbook, it would make the spreadsheet more resilient to errors if we locked all the cells with formulas, shipping data, and totals, so the user can't change them.

To do this, select the cells you want to lock. From the 'data' menu, select 'protected sheets and ranges'.

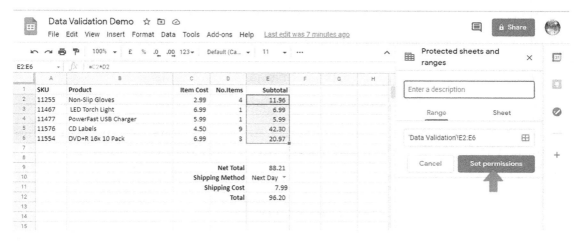

In the panel on the right hand side, add a meaningful description, then click 'set permissions'.

From the dialog box, you can opt to show a warning if any user tries to change the protected cells...

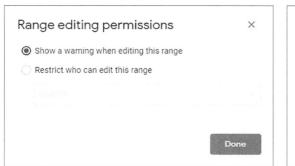
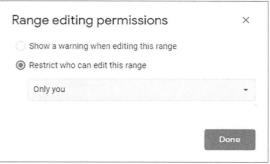

...or you can restrict access to certain users. Such as only yourself.

To set permissions for a group, such as a select group of editors, select 'restrict who can edit this range'. From the drop down box, select 'custom'

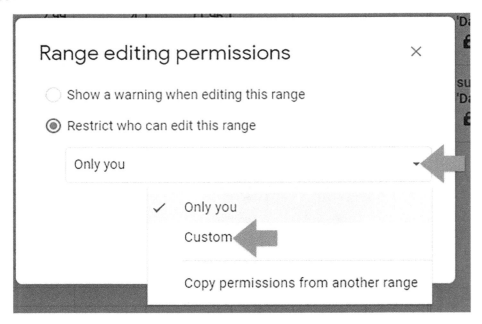

Here, you can set it to yourself only, or select 'custom' to add other people. Enter their email addresses (note they'll need google accounts to be able to edit).

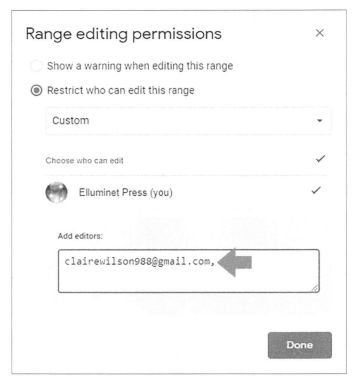

If you've given access to someone else, you'll see a dialog box. From here, click 'share'. This will send a share link to the person's email address.

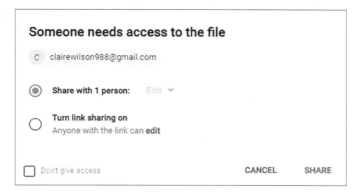

Now, when a user tries to edit a protected cell, they will get an error message.

If you need to edit or delete any protected ranges, select 'protected sheets and ranges' from the 'data' menu. Select the protected range you want from the side panel.

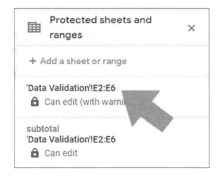

To delete, click the 'trash' icon on the top right. You can also edit any of the details such as the protected cell range, or the permissions.

Sharing & Collaborating

One of Google Sheets main advantages is it's sharing and real-time collaboration features.

This means you can share a file with others allowing them to edit the spreadsheet and add to the project.

You can also communicate with your co-editors, see which changes have been made, and add comments.

In this section, we'll go through collaboration. We'll find out how to share a spreadsheet with other users, how to comment, edit, and work on a sheet with other people.

Have a look at the video resources section. Open your web browser and navigate to the following website.

videos.tips/sharing-googlesheets

Sharing a Sheet

In this demo, lets share a sheet with two other users who will be collaborating on it. The setup is as follows. I will be sharing a sheet from my laptop with Sophie on her chromebook and Claire on her tablet.

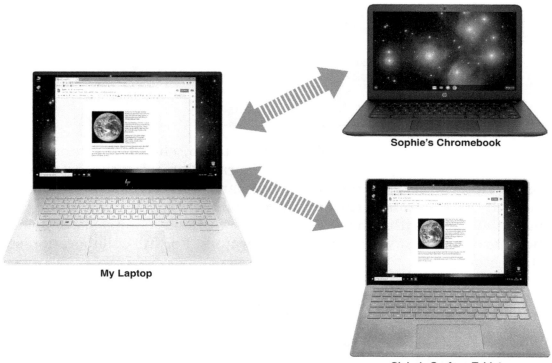

Sophie's Chromebook

My Laptop

Claire's Surface Tablet

These devices could be anywhere in the world that has an internet connection.

To share a sheet, first open the one you want to share, then click the 'share' icon on the top right.

	A	B	C	D	E	F	G	H	I	J	K	L	M	N	O	P	Q	R	S	T	U	V	W
1		22-Apr	29-Apr	6-May	13-May	20-May	27-May	3-Jun	10-Jun	17-Jun	24-Jun	1-Jul	8-Jul	15-Jul	29-Jul	12-Aug	26-Aug	2-Sep	9-Sep	Total	Average Score	Highest Score	
2	Dot	21	21																	42	21.00	21.000	
3	Cathy	21	21																	42	21.00	21.000	
4	Barbara	21	19																	40	20.00	21.000	
5	Shirley		20																	20	20.00	20.000	
6	Barbara	21	21																	42	21.00	21.000	
7	Ann	10	21																	31	15.50	21.000	
8	Emily		0																	0	0.00	0.000	
9	Eva	21	14																	35	17.50	21.000	
10	Norma	8																		8	8.00	8.000	
11	Josie	21	21																	42	21.00	21.000	
12	Joan	19																		19	19.00	19.000	
13	Flo	7	7																	14	7.00	7.000	
14	Lin		0																	0	0.00	0.000	

In the field at the top of the window, enter the email addresses of the people you want to share the spreadsheet with. In this demo, I'm sharing my sheet with Claire and Sophie, so I'd type in their email addresses.

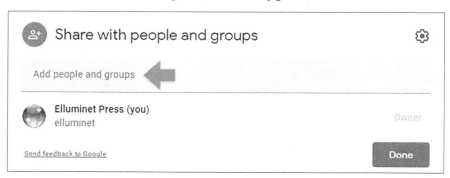

Now set what you want to allow people to do, click the 'editor' drop-down box on the top right. Select a permission from the drop down box. A **viewer** can view the sheet, but can't make changes or share it with others. A **commenter** can make comments, but can't change or share the sheet with others. An **editor** can make changes, comment, and share the sheet with others collaborators. For full collaboration set it to 'editor'.

Make sure 'notify people' is ticked. If you enable 'notify people', all email address will be included in the message.

Enter a message, in the 'message' field.

Click 'send'.

Accepting the Invitation to Collaborate

If someone has shared a spreadsheet with you in Google Sheets, go to your email and open the invitation. Here on Claire's surface tablet, is the invitation to the spreadsheet that was shared with her from my laptop in the previous section. Just click on the 'open in sheets' button. This will open the shared spreadsheet.

The spreadsheet will open in Google Sheets were you can edit the spreadsheet, or write comments and chat with other users.

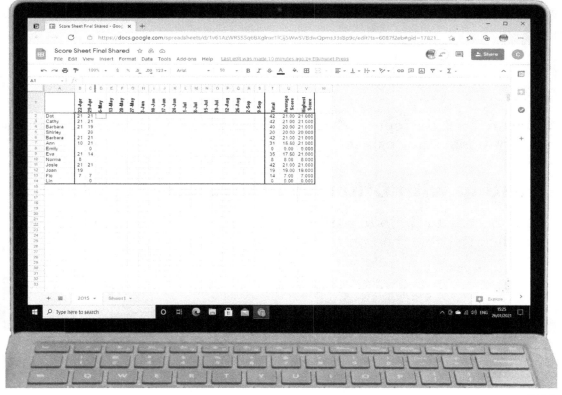

Editing Shared Spreadsheets

All the user's you've shared the spreadsheet with can work on it together.

Making Edits

When you're working on a shared spreadsheet, you'll see each person's edits marked with their username.

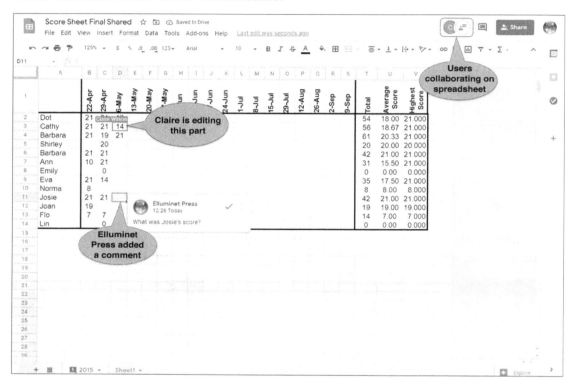

You can edit the spreadsheet as normal, and see everyone else's contributions - they can see the same.

Chatting with Other Collaborators

You can chat to the other users working on your spreadsheet. To do this, click the chat icon on the top right.

Use the chat window on the right hand side, enter your message in the field at the bottom right.

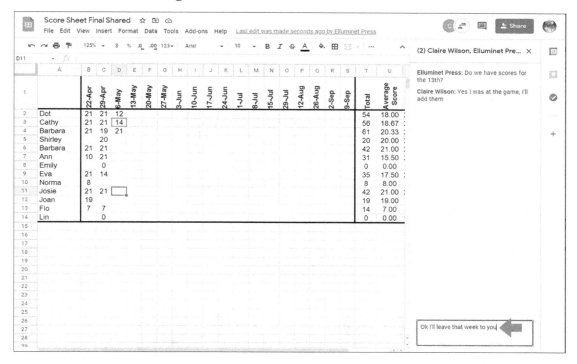

Making Comments

You can also comment on any part of the spreadsheet. To do this, right click on the cell or part of the sheet. From the popup menu, select 'comment'.

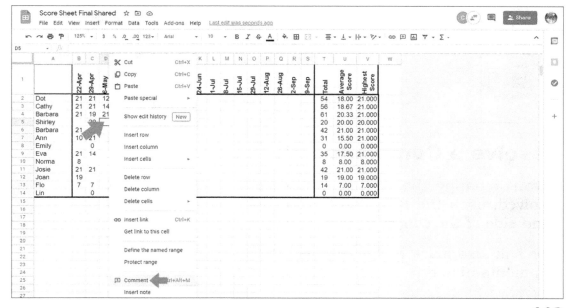

Enter your comment in dialog box. Click 'comment' to post your comment.

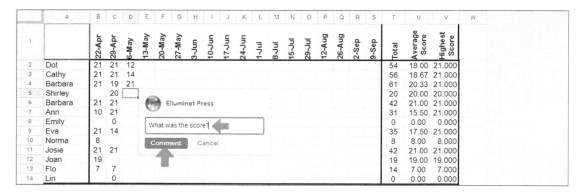

Reply to Comment

Comments are marked with a small orange arrow. Hover your mouse over the arrow to view the comment.

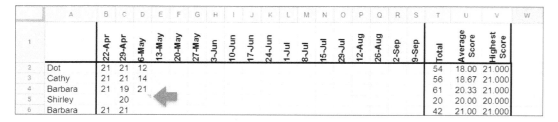

To reply, click on the cell and type your comment into the comment box.

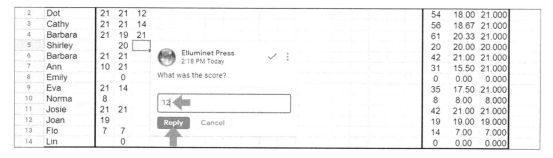

Resolve a Comment

If you're happy the comment has been resolved, click the tick icon on the right hand side of the comment box.

This will also mark it was resolved in the comments history.

Sharing a Link

You can share a link with someone who may or may not even have a Google account. To do this open the spreadsheet you want to share, then click the 'share' icon on the top right.

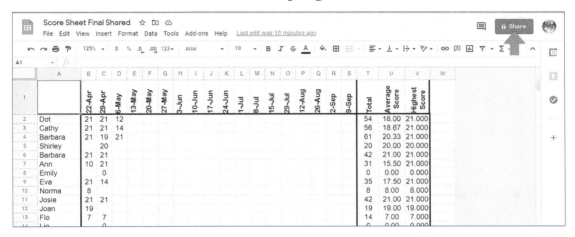

Sharing a Link with Anyone

Sharing a link with anyone means as it's name suggests, anyone who has the link can view the spreadsheet. This is not the most secure way to share a file with someone, so don't use it to share spreadsheets with sensitive information.

Click 'change to anyone with link' in the bottom section.

Google Sheets will generate a link for you.

Set the 'view' permissions. Click on the 'viewer' drop down box, then select an option. If you want the person to just view the spreadsheet, select 'viewer'. If you want the person to be able to edit the spreadsheet, select 'editor'.

Click 'copy' to copy the link to your clipboard.

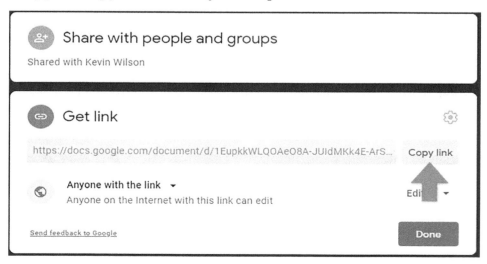

Paste the link into an email or message to send to the person you want to share with. Type a message, then press CTRL - V on your keyboard to paste in the link.

Click 'send' when you're done.

Restricted Links

To generate a link to send to people you've shared a spreadsheet with, click the 'share' icon on the top right.

You'll see a list of people along the top the spreadsheet has been shared with. Click 'change' in the bottom section.

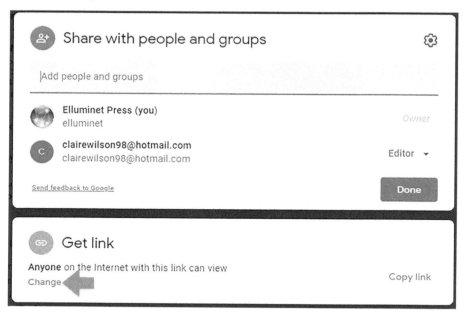

From here, click 'anyone with a link' and change it to 'restricted'.

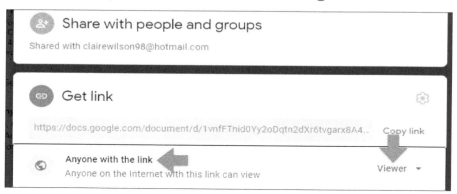

If you want to invite the person to edit the spreadsheet, select the drop down box on the right, change from 'viewer' to 'editor'.

Click 'copy link' on the right hand side, then click 'done'. Paste the link into an email or message.

People without Google Accounts

Sharing a link publicly might not be the best option. If the person doesn't have a Google Account, you can still share the file with them. To do this, open the file then click the 'share' icon on the top right.

Enter the person's email address in the top field and press enter on your keyboard.

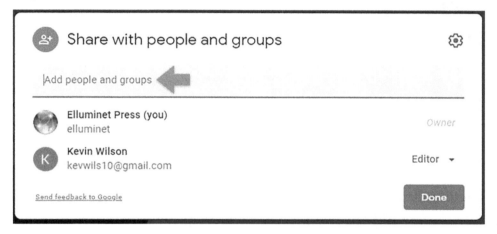

Add a message, then select the permission from the drop down box on the right hand side. Set it to 'editor' if you want this person to be able to edit the spreadsheet.

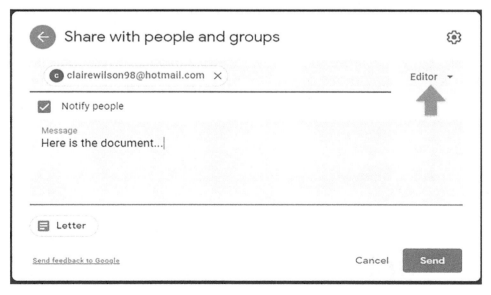

Click 'send', then select 'share anyway' if prompted.

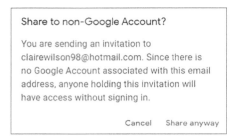

When the other person checks their email, they'll receive an invitation. To view the spreadsheet, click 'open in sheets'.

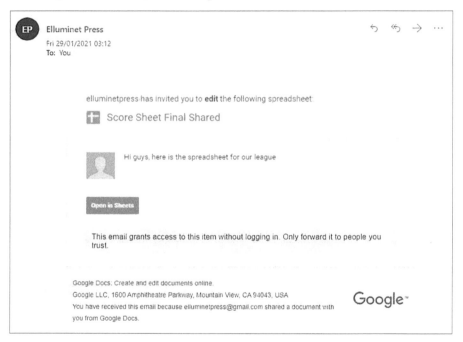

If the person doesn't have a Google Account, they'll need to sign up for one before they can edit the file. When the other person opens the file, they will see a 'sign in' or 'sign up' link on the top right of the screen. To sign up, click 'sign up to edit' and follow the on-screen instructions.

Stop Sharing a File

To stop sharing a file, first open it, then click the 'share' icon on the top right.

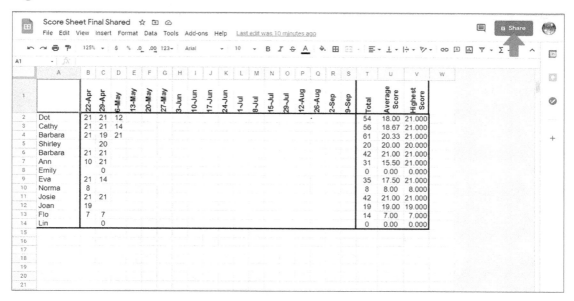

From the 'share with people and groups' section, click the drop down box next to the person you want to remove.

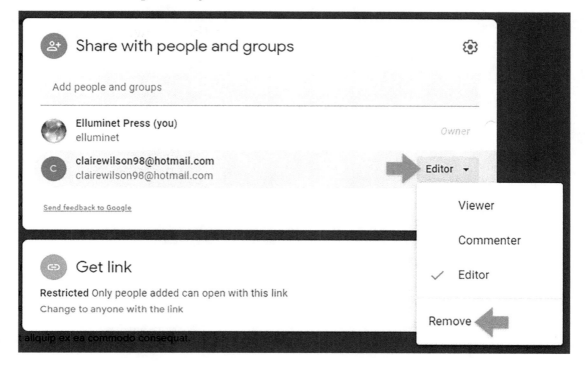

Select 'remove' from the drop down menu. Click 'save' when you're done.

Managing Sheets

In this section, we'll take a look at how to save and open sheets, convert them to other formats, and how to print them out if you need a hard copy.

We'll also take a look at page and print setup, print margins, and how to scale printouts to paper sizes.

Have a look at the video resources section. Open your web browser and navigate to the following website.

`videos.tips/managing-googlesheets`

Opening Spreadsheets

If you're already working on a spreadsheet, you can open another using the 'file' menu. Just select 'open'.

From the 'open' dialog box, navigate to 'My Drive', then select the spreadsheet you want to open.

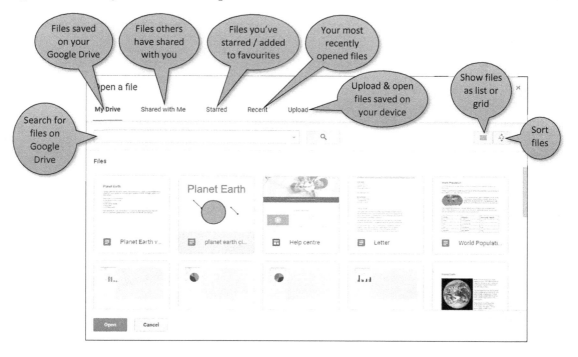

Click 'open' on the bottom left of the dialog box.

If you're opening a spreadsheet from the home screen, click the 'file picker' icon on the right hand side of the screen.

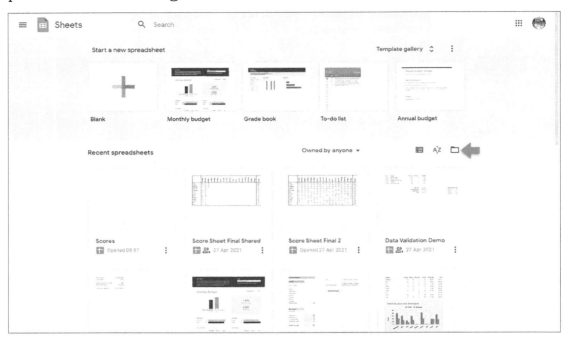

Select the 'My Drive' tab, then click on a file to open. Select a filetype using the drop down box if you're looking for a file other than a Google Spreadsheet.

Click 'open' when you're done.

Uploading Spreadsheets

If you have a spreadsheet saved on your PC, Mac or Laptop, you can upload it

To upload a spreadsheet, click on the 'file picker' icon on the right hand side of the home screen.

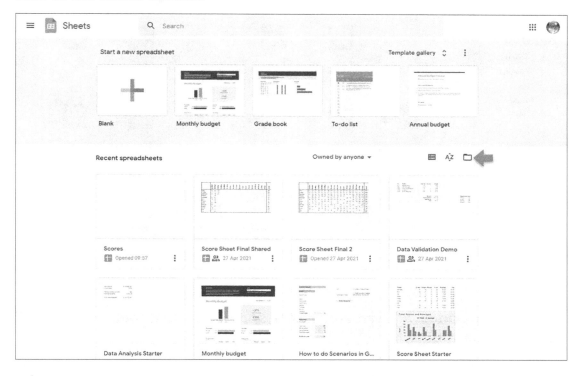

Select the 'upload' tab, then click 'select a file from your device'.

Chapter 9: Managing Sheets

Select a spreadsheet. As we're uploading to Google Sheets, you should upload a Microsoft Excel spreadsheet (.xls or .xlsx), or a text file (such as .csv)

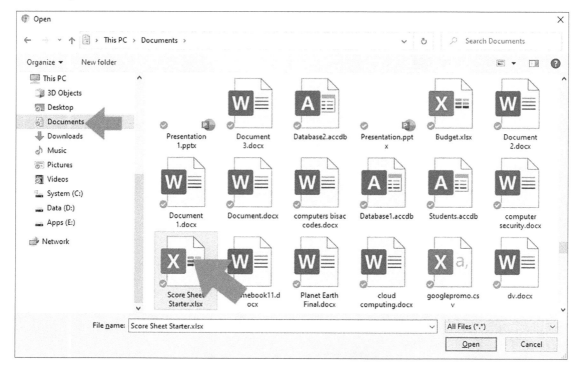

If you've uploaded a Microsoft Excel spreadsheet, Google Sheets will convert it for you.

Downloading & Converting Sheets

If you need to save your spreadsheet for Microsoft Excel, or a PDF, you can do this using the 'spreadsheet download' feature. This is useful if you want to send someone the spreadsheet who uses Microsoft Excel, or if you need to send a report to someone as a PDF.

First open the spreadsheet you want to convert and download. Select the 'file' menu, then go down to 'download'.

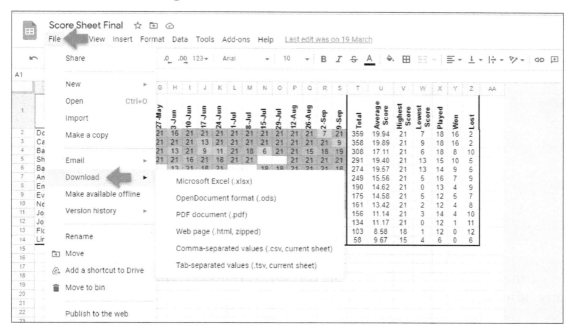

Select the format you want from the slideout menu.

- Use 'Microsoft Excel' if you want to convert and download the spreadsheet as a word spreadsheet.

- Use 'openspreadsheet format' if you want the spreadsheet to be compatible with various word processors, such as Apache OpenOffice or LibreOffice.

- Use 'PDF spreadsheet' if you want to send a read-only version of the spreadsheet such as a sales report to someone else.

- Use 'web page' if you want to convert the spreadsheet to an HTML spreadsheet for a website.

- Use 'comma-separated values' or 'text-separated values' if you want to export the data so the user can import it into another application.

In this example, I'm going to export this spreadsheet as a PDF.

Chapter 9: Managing Sheets

If you're exporting as a PDF, you may need to adjust some settings, such as page orientation, scale or margins. Click 'export'.

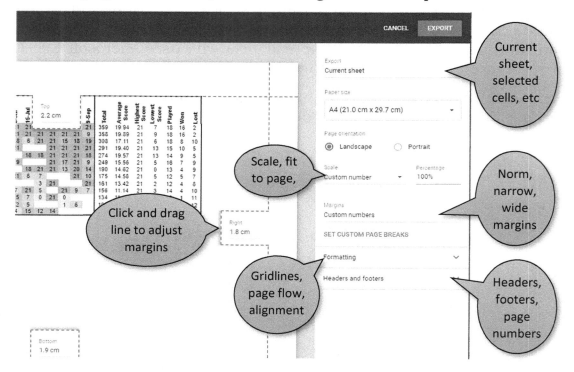

Navigate to the folder on your PC, laptop or mac; give the spreadsheet a name. Here, in the example below, I'm saving this spreadsheet into my 'sheets' folder.

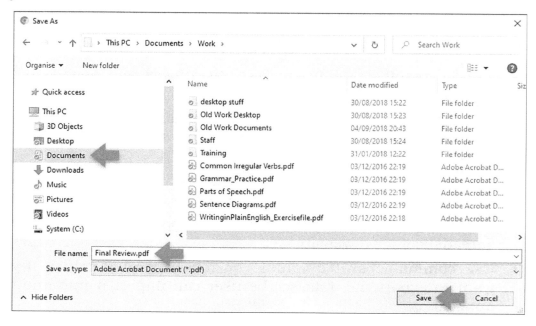

Click 'save'.

Printing Sheets

Once you've finished your spreadsheet, you might need to print it. To do this, make sure your printer is connected and online.

Page Setup & Print

Once you have a spreadsheet open, go to the file menu, on the top left. Select 'print'.

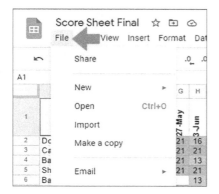 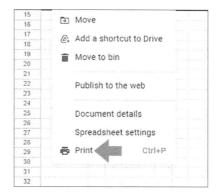

From here, you can select what part of your workbook you want to print such as current sheet, whole workbook (all sheets) or just the selected cells. You can change the paper size: A4, letter, or legal, and the page orientation: landscape or portrait.

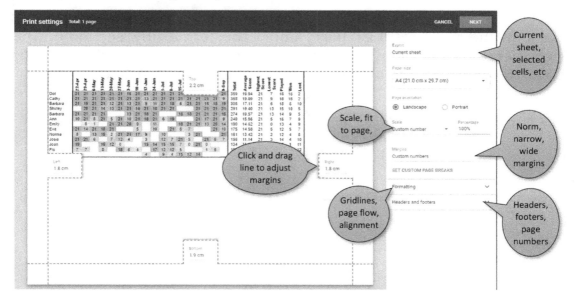

You can set the margins for your spreadsheet. To do this, click and drag the dotted margin lines. You can also use pre-set margins using the 'margins' field on the right hand side.

You can set custom page breaks. Useful if you have a large spreadsheet and you want to divide the pages at specific points. Click 'set custom breaks', then click and drag the dotted line markers to mark your page breaks. In the example below, I want to print the chart on a separate page, so here, I'd drag the bottom dotted line marker between the spreadsheet and the chart. Click 'confirm breaks' when you're done.

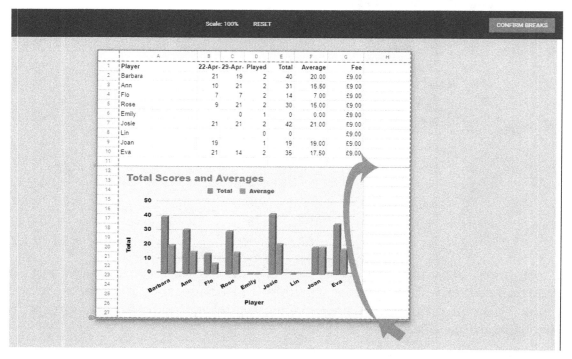

Back on the 'print settings' page, under the 'formatting' section on the right hand side, you can show or hide gridlines and notes, change your page order and set the alignment of the printed spreadsheet.

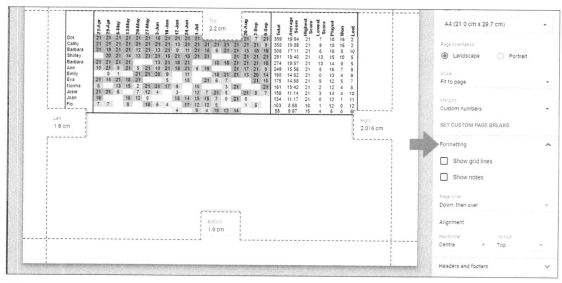

In the headers and footers section, you can add a heading along the top of your spreadsheet, or you can add page numbers. Just select from the presets (page numbers, title etc).

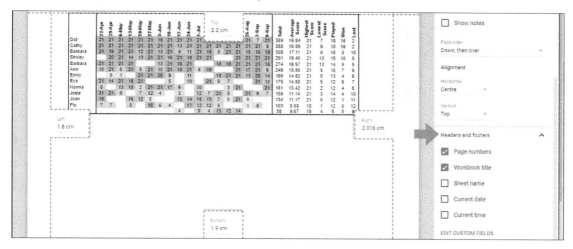

To customise the headers and footers, click 'edit custom fields'. You'll see three fields along the top, and three along the bottom. Click in the fields, then from the popup toolbar, select a field type, eg date, then select a field to enter. Similarly with the footer fields. Click 'confirm' when you're done.

Back on the 'print settings' page, click 'next' to go to print.

In the print dialog box, select your printer, add the number of copies if you want more than one.

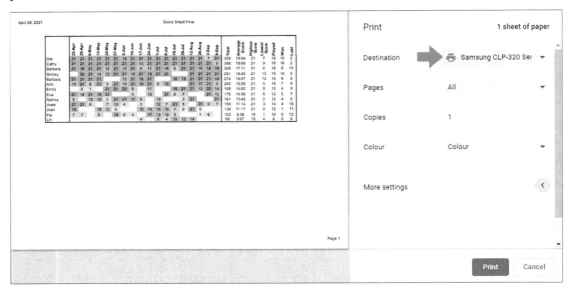

Click 'more settings'. You can also print on both sides if your printer supports this feature. You can adjust the scale and print multiple pages per sheet of paper.

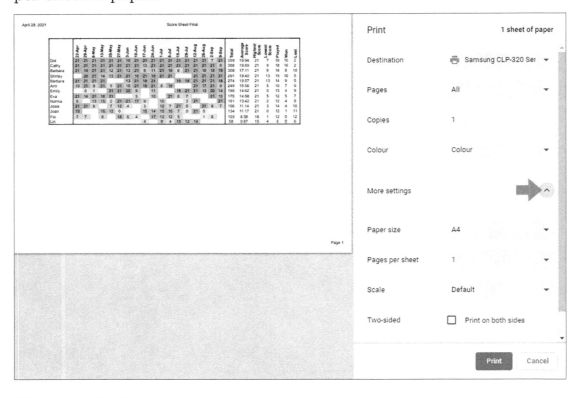

Click 'print' when you're done.

Email as Attachment

You can email your spreadsheet in a variety of formats such as PDF, Word, HTML, plain text and rich text.

To do this, click on the 'file' menu, go down to 'email', then select 'email this file' from the slideout menu.

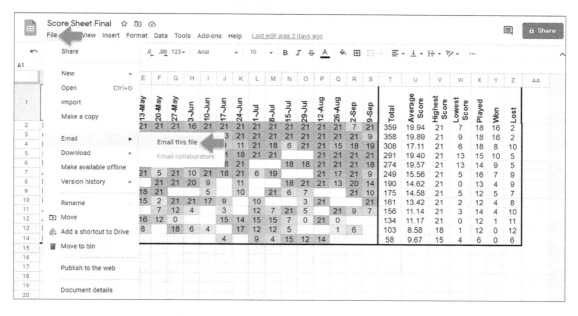

Enter the person's email address in the field at the top, add a message.

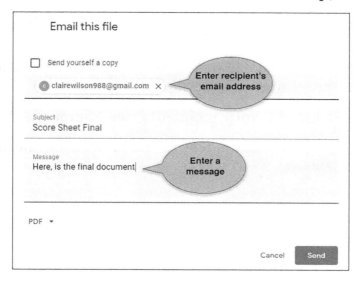

Tick "send yourself a copy" if you want to receive a copy of the email with the spreadsheet attached.

Click 'PDF' on the left hand side.

Select the format using the drop down box on the bottom left.

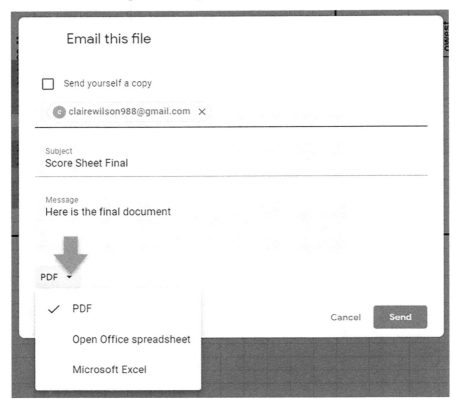

Here, you can select the format you want to send.

- PDF is useful for portability across different platforms, however the recipient won't be able to edit a PDF.

- Open Office spreadsheet is useful for importing into various different spreadsheet programs on other operating systems

- Use Microsoft Excel if your recipient uses Microsoft Office.

This will convert your spreadsheet to the chosen format and attach it to your email message.

Click 'send'.

Spelling & Grammar

To run a spell & grammar check, open the 'tools' menu, select 'spelling and grammar'.

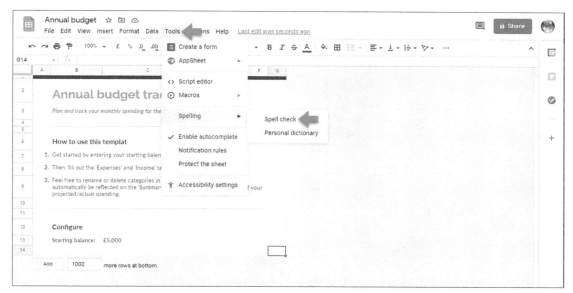

In the dialog box on the right hand side, run through the flagged errors. Here in the example, the spell check as found an error: 'templat' should be spelled 'template'. Click 'change' to correct the error, or 'ignore' to ignore it.

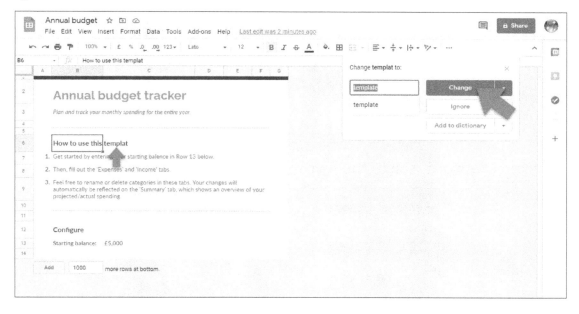

If you know the flagged word is spelled correctly such as a place name, or person's name, click 'add to dictionary'.

If you need to add words to your personal dictionary, open the 'tools' menu, go down to 'spelling', then select 'personal dictionary'

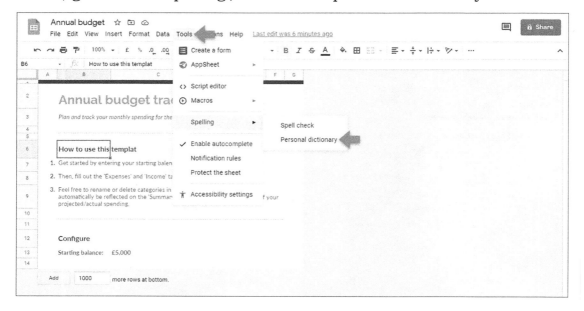

Here, you can add custom words. Type in word, click 'add'.

To remove a word, select the word in the list, click the trash icon.

Click 'ok'.

Add Ons

You can expand Google Sheet's functionality with addons. These add ons are developed mostly by third party developers. You'll find addons for goal seek, scenario managers, functions, accounting and finance as well as sales projections and analytics.

Install

To install an addon, open the 'addons' menu, then select 'get addons'.

Use the search bar along the top to find an addon you want to install.

Or click on the hamburger icon on the top left, then select a category to browse through.

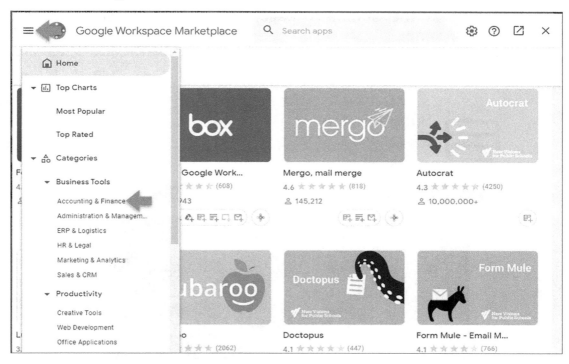

Chapter 9: Managing Sheets

Select an addon to install.

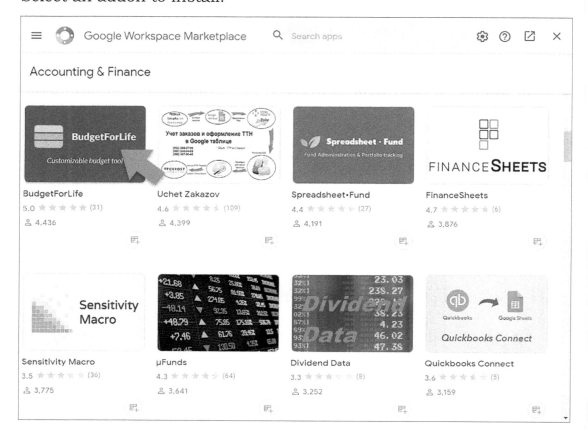

Click 'install' on the summary page. Then click 'continue' on the confirmation prompt.

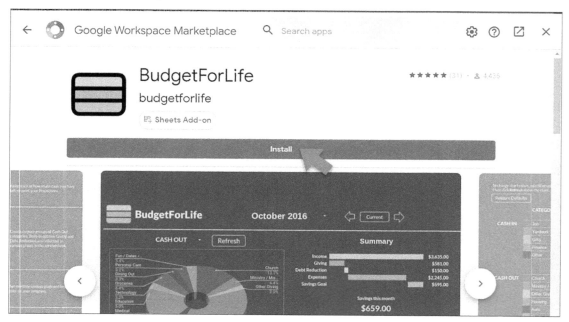

Choose your Google Account... Then click 'allow'.

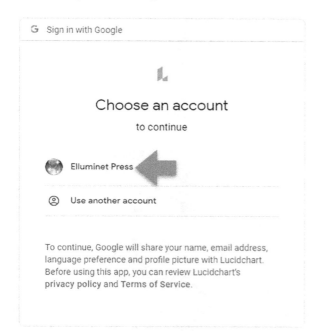

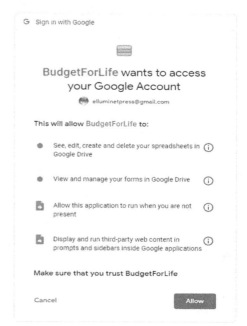

You'll find the addon in the 'addons' menu.

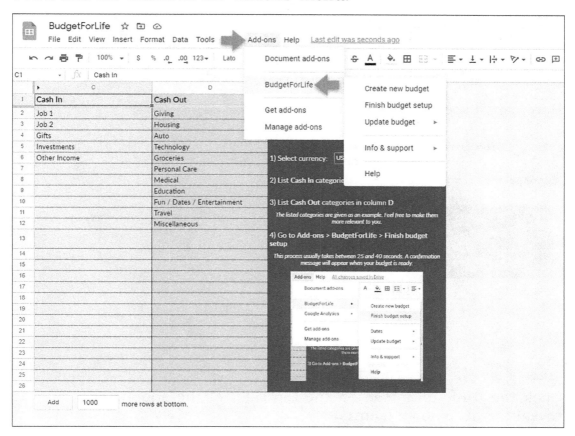

Manage Addons

To manage your addons, open the 'addons' menu then select 'manage addons'.

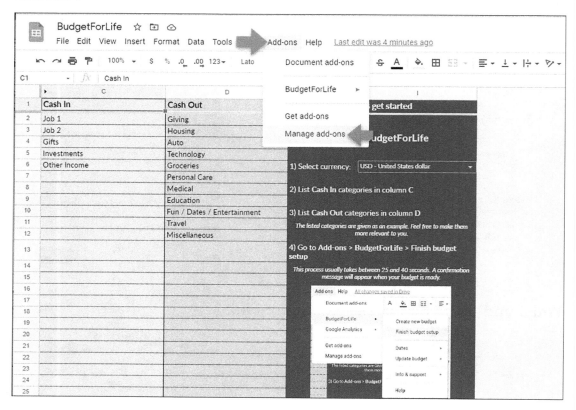

Here, you'll see all the addons you've installed.

Click the three dots icon on the top right of the addon thumbnail to reveal the drop down menu.

Here, you can uninstall the addon.

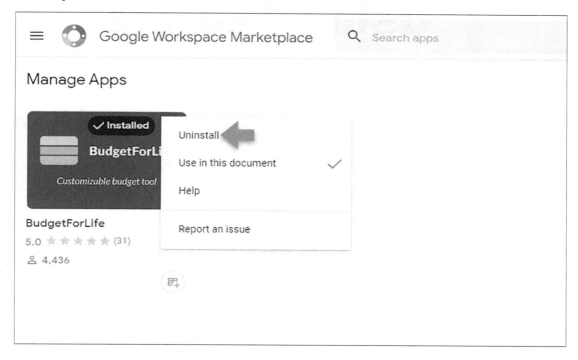

You can also turn add-ons on or off at any time. Click 'use in this document to turn' the add-on on or off.

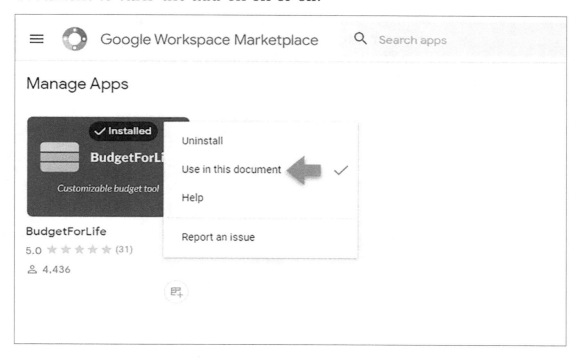

This will disable the addon for the sheet you currently have open.

Using Tablets

You can use Google Sheets on a tablet or phone. You can download the app for an iPhone/iPad, or for an android phone or tablet.

In this section, we'll take a look at how to get started with Google Sheets on a tablet using the app.

We'll go through downloading and installing the app on your tablet, then take a look at some basics on how to open spreadsheets, format text, add tables and images.

Download Google Sheets

To download the Google Sheets app, open the Google Play Store on an android device, or the App Store on an iPhone/iPad. In this demo, I will be using an iPad.

Open the Apps Store, then search for Google Sheets. Tap 'get' to install.

Getting Started

Once Google Sheets has installed itself, you'll find the icon on your home screen. Tap on it to launch the app.

The first time you run the app, you'll need to sign in with your Google Account. To do this, tap the 'sign in' icon on the bottom left.

Enter your Google Account email address and password.

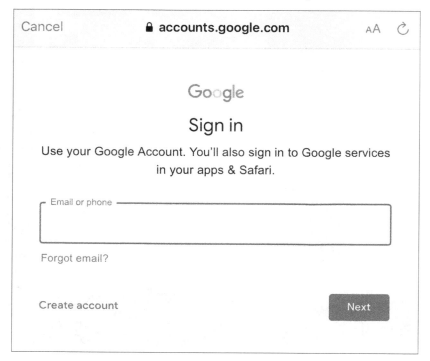

You'll land on the Google Sheets home screen. Let's take a look around. Along the top you'll see an icon to open the sidebar, a search field, file selection field, and your profile icon on the right to change your Google Account Settings.

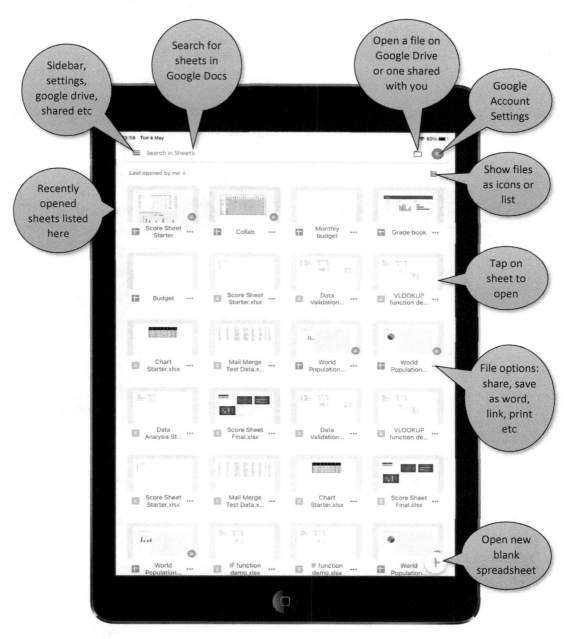

Select a spreadsheet from the recently used list, or click the plus icon on the bottom right, then select 'new spreadsheet' from the popup to open a blank spreadsheet. In this example, I'm going to open a blank spreadsheet.

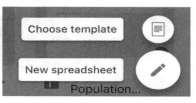

Give the spreadsheet a meaningful name, then tap 'create'.

Once you've opened your spreadsheet, you'll land on the editing screen. Tap in a cell to reveal the toolbar along the top.

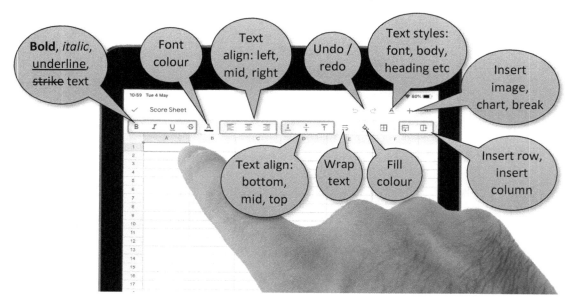

At the bottom of the screen, you'll see your on screen keyboard.

Formatting Text

To enter and format data first open your spreadsheet, then tap the 'edit' icon on the bottom right of the screen.

Next you need to select the cells you want to format. To do this, double-tap on the location in the spreadsheet you want to format. You'll see a blue marker appear on the cell

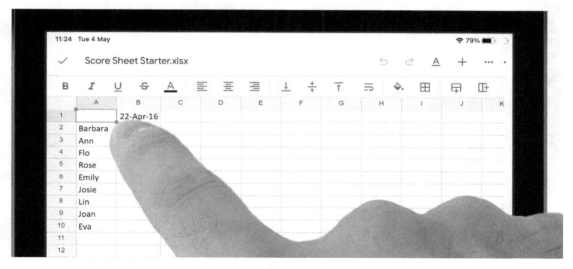

Use your finger to move the blue markers so they highlight the cells you want.

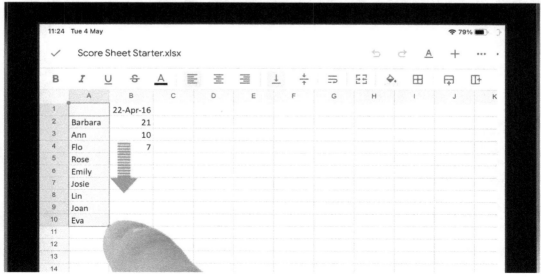

Tap the format icon on the top right. From the drop down menu select the 'text' tab. Here, you can select **bold**, *italic*, underlined, ~~striketext~~, superscript and subscript. Underneath you can change the text style, font typeface, font size, and text colour. Just tap on the option you want to apply to your selected cells.

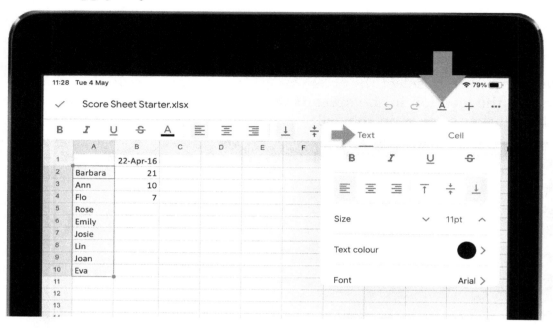

Formatting Cells

To add borders, colour cells, merge cells, or wrap text, select the cells you want to format, then tap the format icon.

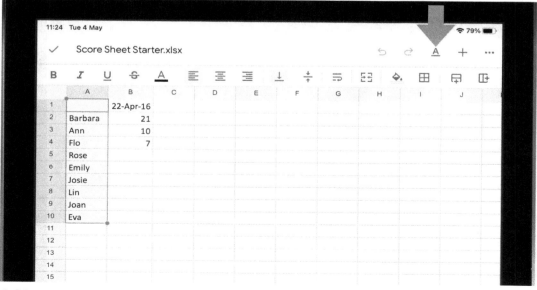

Select the 'cell' tab on the top of the drop down dialog box. Here, you can adjust the cell fill colour, add borders, wrap text, merge cells, as well as change the number format to number, text, currency, date, scientific notations and so on.

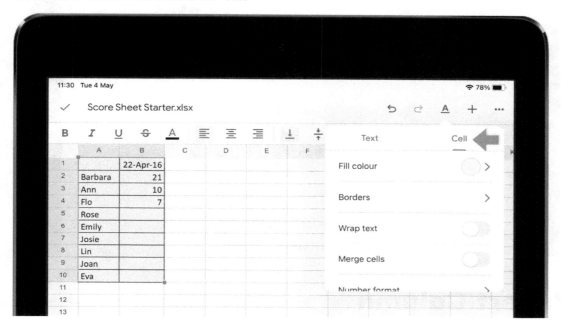

Insert Row

In our score sheet, lets add a row between 'rose' and 'emily'. To do this, tap in the row 'rose' is in.

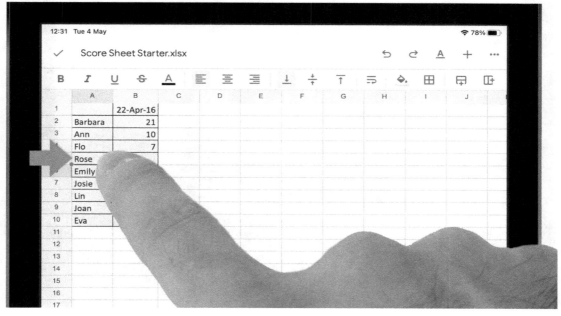

From the toolbar along the top of the screen, tap on the 'add row' icon.

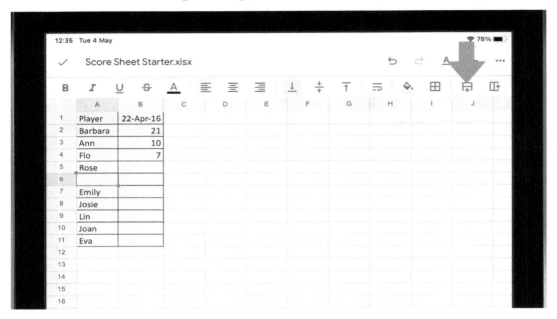

Insert Column

In our score sheet, lets add a column between 'player' and the date. To do this, tap in the column 'player' is in.

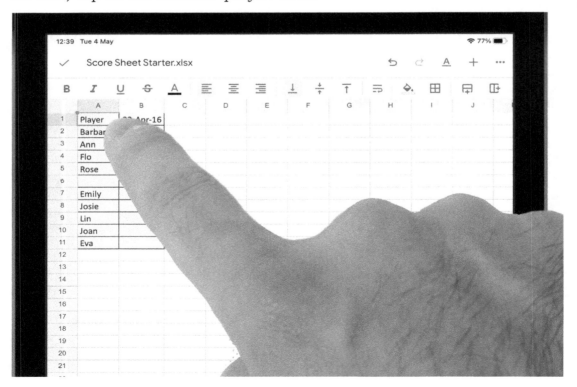

Tap the 'format' icon on toolbar along the top of the screen, then select the 'insert column' icon.

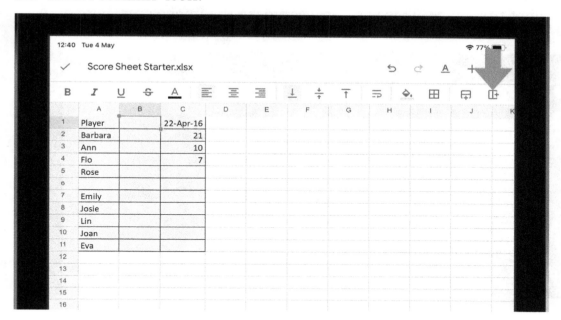

Insert Images

You can insert images saved in your photos on your tablet or directly from your camera. To do this, tap the line in your spreadsheet where you want the image to appear. Tap the 'plus' icon on the top right, then select 'image' from the drop down menu.

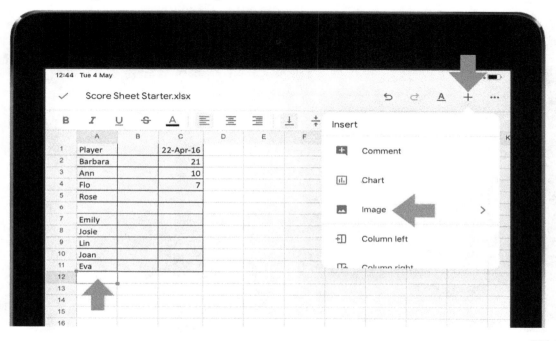

Select whether you want the image to float over the cells, or if you want the image to be inserted into the selected cell. Select 'image over cells' to float the image. This way, you can drag the image anywhere on your spreadsheet.

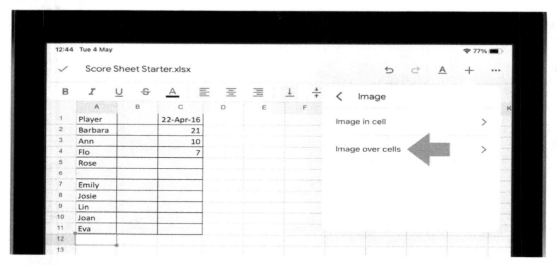

Select 'from photos' to select an image from your photo albums, or select 'from camera' to take one with your tablet's on-board camera.

Select an image to insert...Tap 'add'.

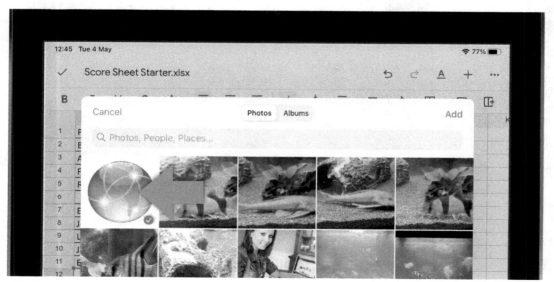

Resize Image

To resize an image, select it in your spreadsheet. You'll notice a border appear around the image appear. On the top left and bottom right, you'll see resize handles.

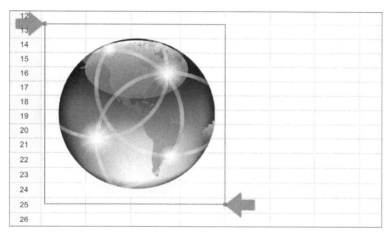

Tap and drag these handles to resize.

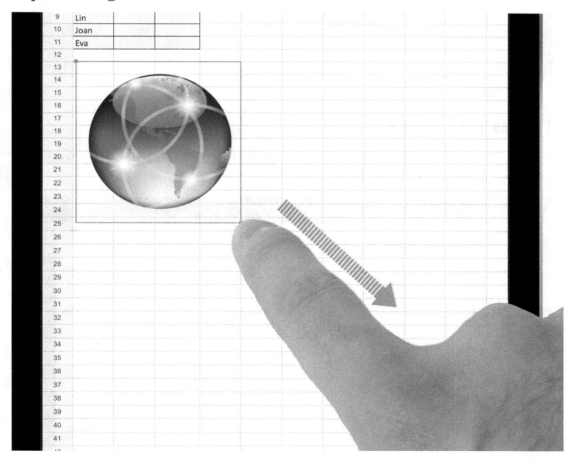

Moving Images

To move your image into position, tap on it to select, then tap and drag the image into the new position.

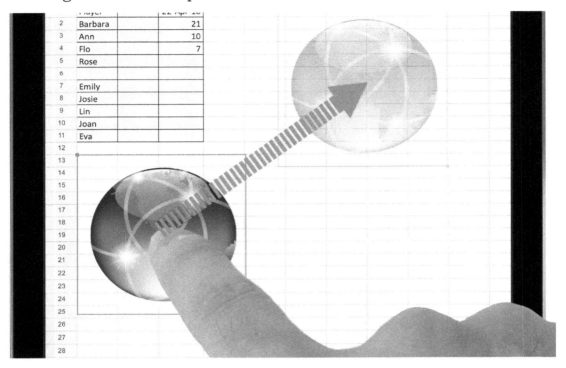

Insert Chart

First, select the cells to include in the chart. Tap and drag the blue marker around the cells.

Tap the 'plus' icon on the top right of the screen, select 'chart'.

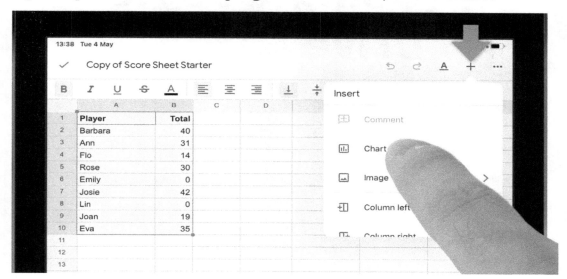

Google Sheets will create a chart from your selected cells.

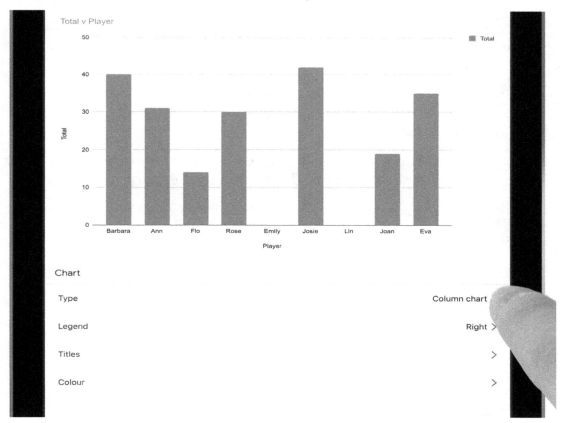

Tap on chart 'type', then select a chart from the options. You can also adjust the legend, titles and colour. Give them a try and see what happens.

Using Google Drive

Google Drive is a cloud storage and synchronization service developed by Google that allows users to store files and synchronize them across multiple devices including Windows, Mac, and chromebook, as well as Android and iPad/iPhone.

You get 15 GB of space on your Drive for free but you can subscribe to various storage plans to suit your needs.

Have a look at the video resources section. Open your web browser and navigate to the following website.

videos.tips/google-drive

Opening Google Drive

Once you've created your Google Account, you can access Google Drive in any web browser (ideally chrome), or from the Google Drive App if you're using a tablet or phone

On the Web

To access Google Drive on the web, open your web browser, then navigate to the following website.

`drive.google.com`

The App

If you're using Google Drive on a tablet or phone, open the app store then download Google Drive if you haven't already done so.

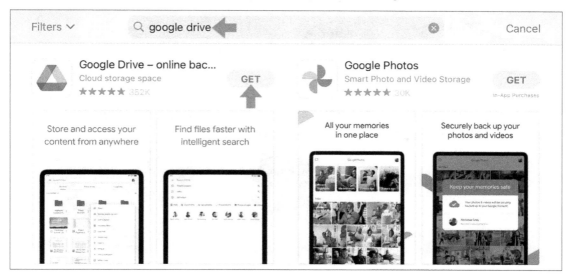

You'll find the Google Drive app on your home screen.

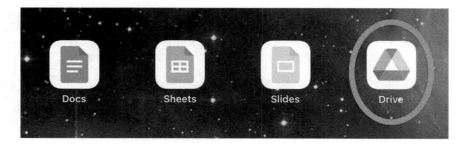

Just tap on the icon to start the app

Getting Around Google Drive

Once you sign into Google Drive using your web browser, you'll land on the home screen. Let's take a look. Down the left hand side panel you'll see some options.

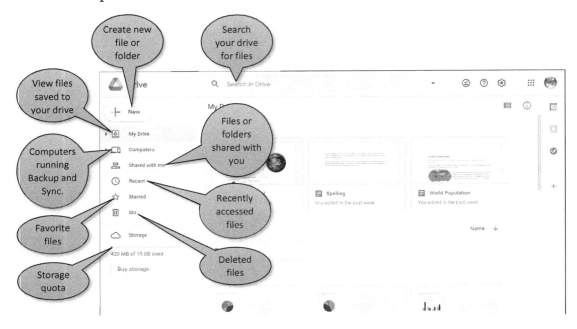

In the main screen, you'll see your 'my drive' view with a list of all the files and folders you've saved to your drive.

If you select a file, you'll see an icon panel appear on the top right. Here, you can create a shareable link, share the file, preview the file or delete the file.

Select the 'more options' icon and you can open the selected file with another app, add a shortcut to your drive sidebar, move the file to another folder, make the file available offline, rename the file, view the file's details, make a copy and download the file for use in another application such as Word, Excel, etc.

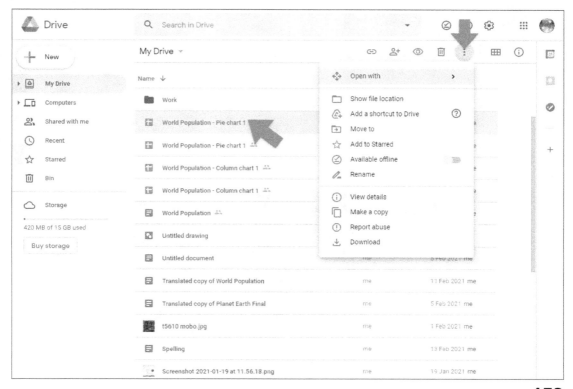

If you're using the app on your phone or tablet, things look a little different. To see all your files and folders, tap the 'files' icon on the right hand side of the icon panel along the bottom of the screen. View your files as icons as shown below - tap the 'view as' icon on the top right.

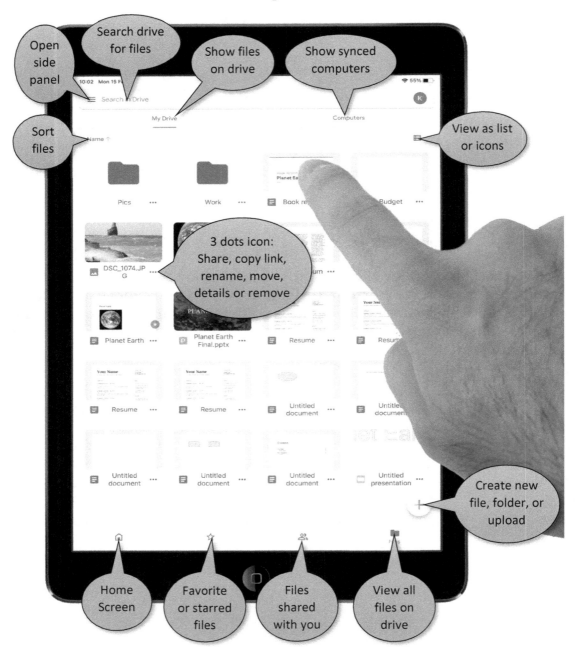

Tap on a file to open it up. Tap the three dots icon on the bottom right of each thumbnail icon to view actions you can take on that file, such as share a link, rename, view details, or delete. Tap the large plus icon on the bottom right to create a new folder or file.

Sync Files with your Computer

You can sync files with your PC, chromebook, mac, phone or tablet.

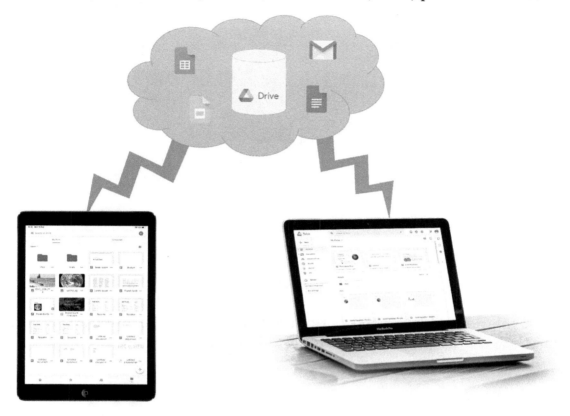

To sync files between your computers and Google Drive, you'll need to download and install the Google Drive for Desktop or Backup and Sync utility. To do this open your web browser and navigate to the following website.

`www.google.com/drive/download`

Google Drive for Desktop

Google Drive for desktop (formerly known as Drive File Stream) is best suited for organisations using Google Drive or Team Drive to share files amongst multiple users working in collaboration. You can't use this version with individual Google Accounts.

Backup and Sync

Backup and Sync is the consumer version of the utility and is aimed at home and individual users.

To install backup and sync, scroll down the installation web page to the 'individual' section. Click 'download'.

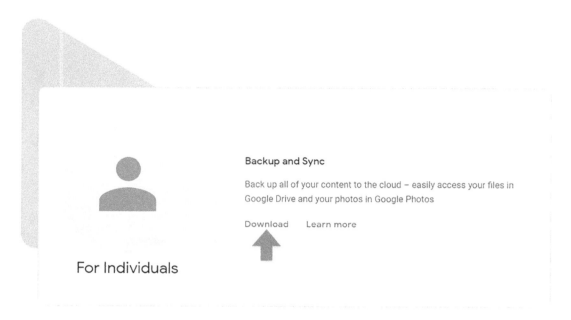

Click the download on the bottom left of your screen to begin. If you don't see a prompt, you'll find the utility in your downloads folder.

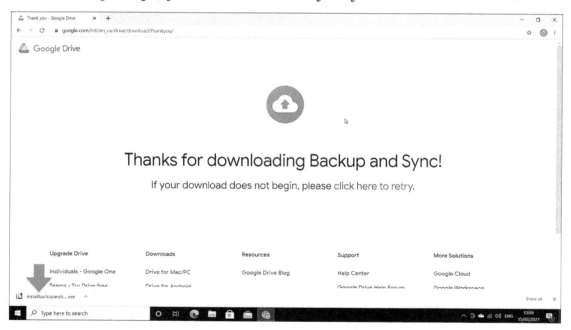

Follow the prompts on the screen to begin the setup.

The utility will download and install on your computer. After a few seconds, you'll see the install wizard appear.

Click 'get started'

Sign in with your Google Account email address and password.

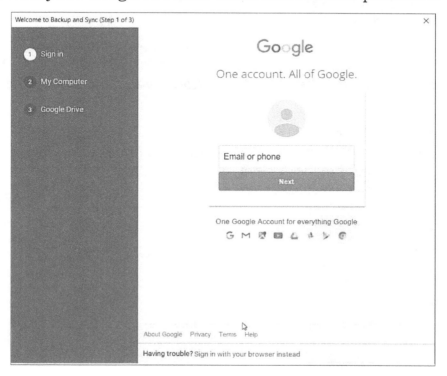

Click 'next'.

Select any folders on your computer you want to backup to Google Drive. This could be your documents folder, pictures, or any folder you save files to. These folders appear in the 'computers' section on Google Drive.

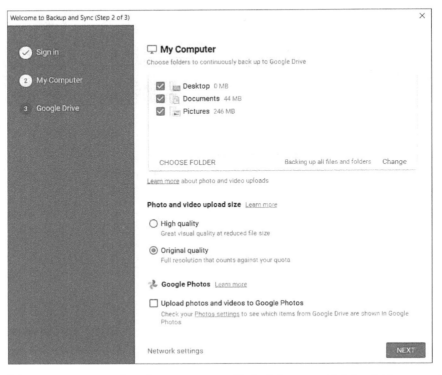

If any folders you use don't appear, click 'choose folder' then select the folder to add. You don't have to select any folders to backup and you can untick all the suggestions if you don't want to backup files. Click 'next'.

Select 'sync my drive to this computer'. Most of the time you can leave this in the default location, but if you need to change the folder or drive Google Drive syncs files to, select 'change' then choose a folder.

Select 'sync everything in my drive', then click 'start'.

You'll notice some icons appear on your desktop, these are shortcut icons to Google Drive, Docs, Sheets, etc.

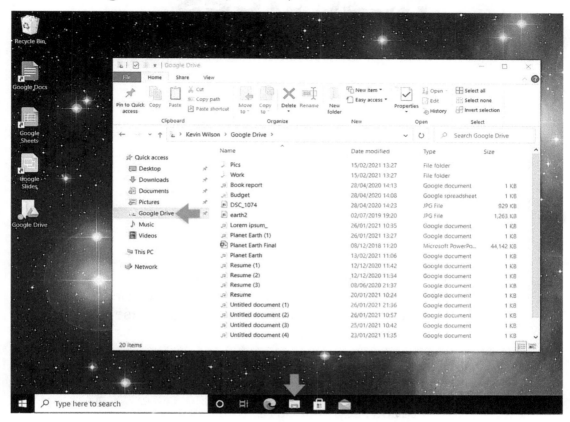

You'll also find the Google Drive folder in File Explorer. This is where you should save new files that you want to sync across to Google Drive and be available on all your devices.

You'll also see the backup and sync utility in the system area on the bottom right of the screen. Here you can view recently synced files as well as change settings.

The icons along the top of the window allow you to view Google Drive folder in File Explorer, open Google Drive in a web browser, open Google Photos.

The three dots icon on the top right, will reveal a drop down menu, where you can change settings, pause sync, or change account.

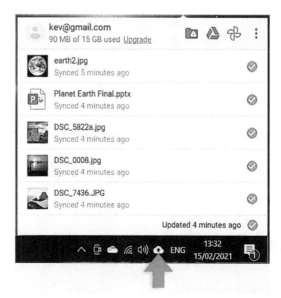

Resources

To help you understand the procedures and concepts explored in this book, we have developed some video resources and app demos for you to use, as you work through the book.

To find the resources, open your web browser and navigate to the following website

`videos.tips/google-sheets`

At the beginning of each chapter, you'll find a website that contains the resources for that chapter.

Video Resources

The video resources are grouped into sections for each chapter in the book. Click the thumbnail link to open the section.

When you open the link to the video resources, you'll see a thumbnail list at the bottom.

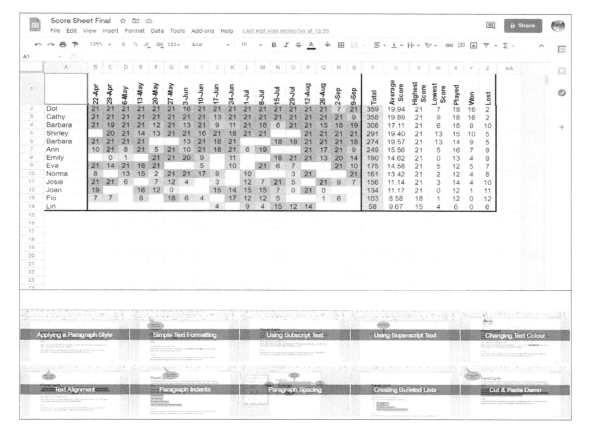

Appendix A: Resources

Click on the thumbnail for the particular video you want to watch. Most videos are between 30 and 60 seconds outlining the procedure, others are a bit longer.

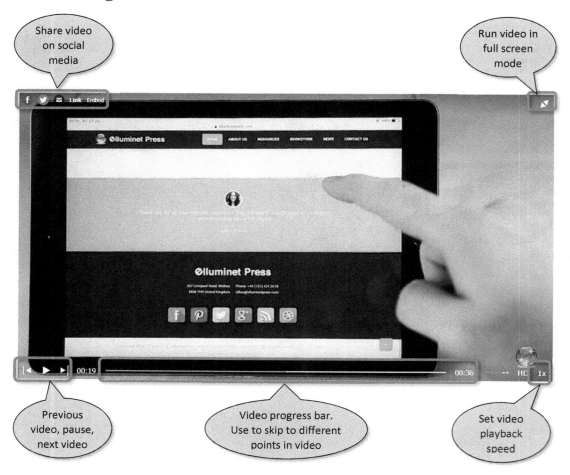

When the video is playing, hover your mouse over the video and you'll see some controls...

File Resources

To save the files into your documents folder, right click on the icons above and select 'save target as' (or 'save link as', on some browsers). In the dialog box that appears, select the 'Documents' folder, then click 'save'.

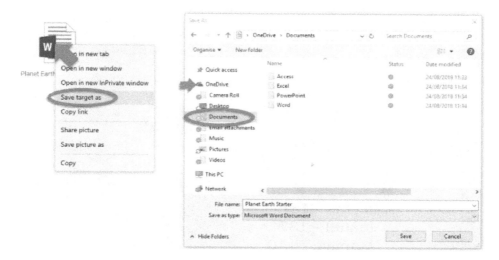

The sample images are stored in a compressed zip file. To download the zip file, right click on the zip icon on the page above, 'Sample Images. zip. Select 'save target as' (or 'save link as', on some browsers) and save it into your 'pictures' folder.

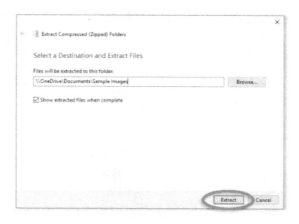

Once you have downloaded the zip file, go to your 'pictures' folder, right click on the zip file, and select 'extract all' from the menu. From the dialog box that appears click 'extract'. This will create a new folder in your pictures called 'sample images'. You'll find the images used in the examples in the books.

Index

D

Index